PANCHAYATI RAJ
FROM
LEGISLATION TO MOVEMENT

Panchayati Raj
From
Legislation to Movement

George Mathew

Concept Publishing Company
New Delhi - 110 059

ISBN 81-7022-517-5

First Published 1994
Reprinted 1995, 2002

Published and Printed by
Ashok Kumar Mittal
Concept Publishing Company
A/15-16, Commercial Block, Mohan Garden
New Delhi-110059 (India)
Phones: 5648039, 5649024
Fax: 091-(11)-5648053
E-mail: publishing@conceptpub.com

Earlier versions of parts of this book, appearing as my contributions to various newspapers, are acknowledged below:
The Hindu: "Panchayati Raj: The Will is Missing," 12 December 1991; "Need for Healthy Connections," 13 December 1991; "Onslaught on Panchayati Raj" (I & II), 7-8 July 1992; "From Legislation to Movement," 9 January 1993; "Panchayats: Orissa Leads the Way," 27 March 1993; "Karnataka Puts the Clock Back," 19 April 1993; "Will the Congress Usher in Panchayati Raj?" 7 June 1993; "Panchayat Elections in West Bengal" (I & II), 1-2 July 1993. *The Hindustan Times:* "Panchayat Poll in Karnataka," 9 February 1987; "Who's Afraid of Local Polls?" 21 April 1988; "Panchayati Raj: What Government Should Do" 17 January 1990; "Kerala Poll: Its Significance," 21 February 1991. *Indian Express*: "Dismal Record of Panchayati Raj," 2 October 1987; "A Vote for Women in Orissa," 20 July 1992. *Yojana:* "Panchayati Raj: The Second Phase," 26 January 1989.

In addition, I have used my "Introduction" to *Panchayati Raj in Karnataka Today: Its National Dimensions,* as well as the "Introduction" and chapter three from *Panchayati Raj in Jammu and Kashmir* for this book.

COVER PICTURES: 1. The Parliament (courtesy, *The Times of India.*) 2. A rare archival photo of the Dandi March. Gandhiji is seen going in the opposite direction (courtesy, Nehru Memorial Museum Library).

To the memory of Abdul Nazir Sab
who said goodbye so early,
leaving his work on panchayati raj unfinished

Contents

Contents

Foreword

The constitution has done its duty. It is now for the people to ensure that the purpose and promise of democratic decentralisation, embodied in the 73rd amendment, is delivered. The title of this book, *Panchayati Raj: From Legislation to Movement*, eloquently communicates this message.

Though this is not the occasion to harp on the past, it is necessary to remind ourselves that the essence and intent of the constitution has been defied by those who have occupied the seats of power, in spite of their taking an oath to protect and preserve it. The basic directive of the constitution in respect of universalisation of elementary education, abolition of untouchability, creating conditions for the fulfilment of the right to work, to means of livelihood and to equality between men and women, prevention of concentration of economic power in fewer hands, have all remained not only unrealised, but unpromoted by the state, ever since the adoption of the constitution in 1950.

The belief that panchayats, duly endowed with autonomy and the resources for flourishing as units of self-government as envisaged in the 73rd amendment, will come into their own simply with the passing of the legislation, would be naive, to say the least. If one thing can make a dynamic difference to this proposition, it is a resolute movement by the people to ensure that the governance of this country is substantially democratised.

This book is not meant to be the last word on the subject but only an initial signal to the people to rally themselves for the challenge placed in their hands by the constitutional amendment. Should this signal command the notice of different sections of the society, even in a small measure, the labour of the author of this eminently well-documented, well-written and very readable volume will be more than justified.

Governance of India, as even the blind can see, is under tremendous pressure. In my view, what India requires is more democracy rather than less democracy, as some skeptics seem to believe. If India is not self-governed, to the utmost possible extent, in its villages, talukas and districts, it will become ungovernable.

It is time for all men and women to come to the aid of good governance–to sustain and to put meaning into the freedom we obtained from foreign rule after a long and non-violent struggle.

L. C. Jain

Preface

Although we, in India, have a great legacy and tradition of village governance system (the panchayats), in its effective formulation and articulation we have been found wanting. Even after independence, despite all the commitment of nationalist leaders for *Grama Swaraj* (village self-government), the Constituent Assembly was not categoric about it. Thus panchayats found a place only in the Directive Principles of State Policy, leaving it to the good will of individual states to give the system meaning and content. Starting from the Community Development programme and National Extension Service and passing through innumerable committees and commissions, indeed, panchayati raj has had a chequered evolution, culminating in the 73rd constitutional amendment.

The political non-commitment and lack of constitutional safeguards paved the way for strengthening the tendency towards centralisation that characterised Indian polity in its early period. The centralisation of political authority reached its peak during the 1980s. Unprecedented destabilisation in the states, all-round loss of faith in democratic institutions, deteriorating living conditions of rural people, growing parochialism and rise of militancy were some of the turbulent manifestations. Enlightened political opinion began to voice its anguish over these trends, pinpointing decentralisation of power and reviving of local government system as the answer to the malady that was overtaking our society and politics.

The silver lining in the mid-eighties in the otherwise gloomy horizon was the bold experiment of decentralisation of power by two states–West Bengal and Karnataka. These experiments, in reality, pushed the idea of real, grassroots-level democracy as a priority on the national agenda. Thus, power to the people through local governments began to be accepted as the answer to the questions of meaningful democracy at the grassroots level, social and economic development of rural and urban areas, as well as national integration.

My interest in panchayati raj, local government, and the overarching subject of decentralisation of power arose from my conviction that these are the instrumentalities to meet effectively the challenges facing our polity and society. The experiences of other countries also confirmed me in my conviction. Thus I began to reflect on these issues and this book is the result of that process. The papers and articles I wrote since then in the *Indian Express*, the *Hindustan Times*, *Yojana* and the *Hindu*, and others taken from some of my edited works on panchayati raj in response to events and developments in last seven years form the basis of this book. I feel that if the mid-eighties were a period of gloom in regard to local bodies, the mid-nineties could chart a new course. There are imponderables and difficult terrains to traverse. All is not well. I have tried to look at the scenario critically, albeit with optimism. After all, humankind lives on hope.

At this juncture, when serious efforts are being made to implement the 73rd and 74th constitutional amendments, a volume like this may be of some value to understand the issue in proper perspective. Therefore, among the articles published in various newspapers, journals and books, a selection has been made, revised and thematically presented in this volume.

George Mathew

Part One

The Historical Background

1

The National Setting

There is no other socio-political programme launched by the government in independent India which has generated as much enthusiasm and participation of the people as the panchayati raj institutions (PRIs).[1] But the irony is that when the potential of the panchayati raj institutions was reaching its peak, the system developed a tendency for imminent collapse.

The story of the ups and downs of panchayati raj in India was well brought out by the Asoka Mehta committee[2] in 1978 when it identified three phases in the life of panchayati raj, starting from its inception till 1977: a) the phase of ascendancy, 1959 to 1964; b) the phase of stagnation, 1965 to 1969; and c) the phase of decline, 1969 to 1977. After 1977, the decline was even more rapid. In fact today, in most states, the panchayati raj system has become moribund. For this sorry pass, three arguments could be put forward. First, panchayati raj collapsed due to the weight of its own inner contradictions. Second, the system was inherently sound but became emaciated because of certain conditions beyond anyone's control. Third, the ruling elites deliberately "killed" it. The plausibility of the third argument is evident as we look into the issue analytically. How and why were the panchayati raj institutions destroyed nationwide?

Traditional Panchayats

It is widely recognised that village communities characterised by agrarian economies had existed in India from the earliest times. The Russian *mir,* the German *mark,* and the medieval **manor** of England could be considered the counterparts of Indian village *panchayats* (an assembly of five persons). The important characteristics of these panchayats, which existed in ancient India, were that they had been the pivot of administration, the centre of social life, forum for justice, an important economic force and, above all, a focus of social solidarity. So much so, Sir Charles Metcalfe, a British governor in India in the nineteenth century, had called them "the little republics" (*Imperial Gazetteer of India* 1909: 278-79). This does not mean that these "republics" were ideal centres thriving with the democratic participation of all the people. Given the caste-ridden feudal structure of the village society of those days, they left much to be desired. B.R. Ambedkar took this issue to the extreme when he remarked in the Constituent Assembly, "What is the village but a sink of localism, a den of ignorance, narrow-mindedness and communalism?"[3] He went on to say that these village republics had been the ruination of India.

One may not agree with Ambedkar in his depiction of the village republic but what is important here is to guard equally against a romantic view of the ancient village system, especially in relation to the values of equality and democracy. The late Jayaprakash Narayan had perceptively commented, "The old village communities have survived in nothing else than their physical existence. They are no longer living communities acting jointly for the solution of individual or communal problems and for the development of their moral and material life" (quoted in Venkatarangaiya and Pattabhiram 1969).

During the British period, the working village assemblies were kept alive and wherever there was a demand for them they were revived. It is a historical fact that local self-government in India, in the sense of a representative institution accountable to the electorate, was the creation of the British. The government resolution of 18 May 1882, during Lord Ripon's viceregal tenure, providing for local boards consisting of a large majority of elected non-official members and presided over by a non-official chairman, was considered the Magna Carta of local democracy in India. By 1925 eight provinces in British India had passed acts for the establishment of village panchayats.[4] By 1948, twenty native states had enacted village panchayat acts.[5] However, these statutory panchayats covered only a limited number of villages and had, generally, a limited number of functions.

Village Panchayats and the National Movement

In the national movement for political freedom, village panchayats were central to its ideological framework. Gandhi*ji* had categorically defined his vision of village panchayats in the following words:

> My idea of village *Swaraj* is that it is a complete republic independent of its neighbours for its own vital wants and yet interdependent for many others in which dependence is a necessity....The Government of the village will be conducted by the Panchayat of five persons annually elected by the adult villagers, males and females, possessing minimum prescribed qualifications. These will have all the authority and jurisdiction required. Since there will be no system of punishment in the accepted sense, the Panchayat will be the legislature, judiciary and executive combined to operate for its year of office. Any village can become such a republic today without much interference even from the present government whose sole effective connection with the villages is the execution of the village revenue....Here there is perfect democracy based upon individual freedom. The individual is the architect of his own Government (Gandhi 1942).

It is a sad commentary on India's national commitment to democratic decentralisation that despite a history of the village as the basic unit of administration, the nationalist movement's commitment to panchayats, and despite Gandhiji's unequivocal propagation of the ideal, the first draft of India's constitution did not find a place for panchayats in it. Ambedkar attacked the protagonists of villages as units of administration, maintaining that he was surprised that "those who condemn provincialism and communalism should come forward as champions of the village" (Vekatarangaiya and Pattabhiram 1969). But members like Madhava Rau of Mysore countered him, saying, "It is true, some villages are chronically faction-ridden and indulge in petty tyrannies, or remain the strongholds of untouchability. A considerable number are pathetic or even moribund." However, according to him, even if 30 percent could be classed as good, they could not be ignored. He quoted the example of the effort being made by the then popular government in Mysore as "encouraging and in some cases quite gratifying" (Venkatarangaiya and Pattabhiram 1969). The argument of those who pleaded for the inclusion of village panchayats in the constitution finally prevailed albeit in a modest measure. They managed to get a provision included in Part IV of the constitution (in the Directive Principles of State Policy) under Article 40 which, however, is not justiciable: "The State should take steps to organise village panchayats and endow them with such power and authority as may be necessary to enable them to function as units of self-government."

The Gandhians considered panchayati raj both a means as also an end and sincerely believed in its immense potential for democratic decentralisation and for devolving power to the people. Of course, Ambedkar's objection had not been to democratic decentralisation or to the concept of giving power to the people, which would have been the outcome of an ideal panchayati raj system. He was speaking from his experience at the existential level about what a village in India had meant to him and to millions like him. No doubt his perception was as realistic as that of others.

The basic conviction that village panchayats could play an important role in the social transformation and implementation of development programmes could not be ignored so easily and hence we find a provision, at least in the directive principles of the constitution. But the pertinent questions still remain unanswered. Why did panchayati raj not come under the legally enforceable part of the constitution? Why was it not given the constitutional status and recognition it deserved? The answer is that the urban and the rural elite, its representatives in politics (from the time of the national freedom movement onwards), and a bureaucracy conditioned by its class character, had a disdain for the panchayati raj system, and this has ever since remained intact. Whatever genuine attempts were made for the devolution of power, these interests saw to it that these attempts did not succeed. The story of panchayati raj institutions since independence is precisely this.

Notes

1. Panchayati raj is a process of governance; it refers to a system. Etymologically it is derived from Urdu. In one of his meetings with the author, Shri S.K. Dey had disclosed that the term was coined by Jawaharlal Nehru. It is distinct from panchayat raj which connotes government of a local body limited to a geographical area.
2. The Janata government appointed on 12 December 1977 a committee headed by Asoka Mehta to enquire into the working of the panchayati raj institutions, and to suggest measures to strengthen them so as to enable a decentralised system of planning and development to be effective. It is popularly known as the Asoka Mehta Committee (1978) and the report is entitled *Report of the committee on panchayati raj institutions.*
3. B.R. Ambedkar in the Constituent Assembly on 4 November 1948.
4. The eight provinces in British India which passed acts for the establishment of village panchayats were: Madras (Panchayat Act of 1920); Bombay (Village Panchayat Act of 1920), Bengal (Self-Government Act of 1919); Bihar (Self-Government Act of 1920); Central Provinces and Berar (Panchayat Act of 1920); Uttar Pradesh (Village Panchayat Act of 1920); Punjab (Panchayat Act of 1922); Assam (Self-Government Act of 1925).
5. The native states which enacted legislations were the following:
   (i) Cochin Panchayats Regulations Act 1919
   (ii) Holkar State Panchayat Act, 1920.
   (iii) Travancore Village Panchayat Act, 1925.
   (iv) Baroda Village Panchayat Act, 1926.
   (v) Kolhapur Panchayat Act, 1926.
   (vi) Mysore Village Panchayat Act, 1926.
   (vii) Bikaner Village Panchayat Act, 1928.
   (viii) Karauli Village Panchayat Act, 1939.
   (ix) Hyderabad Village Panchayat Act, 1940.
   (x) Mewar Gram Panchayat Act, 1940.
   (xi) Jasdan Village Panchayat Act, 1942.
   (xii) Bhavnagar Village Panchayat Act, 1943.
   (xiii) Porbandar Village Panchayat Act, 1943.
   (xiv) Bharatpur Village Panchayat Act, 1944.
   (xv) Marwar Gram Panchayat Act, 1945.
   (xvi) Wadia State Village Panchayat Act, 1946.
   (xvii) Dharangadhra State Village Panchayat Act, 1946.
   (xviii) Morvi State Village Panchayat Act, 1946.
   (xix) Sirohi Village Panchayat Act, 1947.
   (xx) Jaipur Village Panchayat Act, 1948.

   (See *A Quarterly of the Local Self-Government Institute* 1949: 452-53).

2

The First Generation

After the Community Development project was inaugurated in 1952, those at the helm of affairs realised that without an agency at the village level "which could represent the entire community, assume responsibility and provide the necessary leadership for implementing development programmes," real progress in rural development could not come about (Government of India 1958). The recommendation in the report of the Team for the Study of Community Projects and National Extension Services, headed by Balwantrai G. Mehta, that "public participation in community works should be organised through statutory representative bodies," [1] gave a fillip to the prevailing nationwide sentiments. Later, the National Development Council affirmed the basic principles of democratic decentralisation and left it to the states to work out the structures suitable to each state.

Rajasthan was the first state to inaugurate panchayati raj and Prime Minister Jawaharlal Nehru hailed it as "the most revolutionary and historical step in the context of new India" (quoted in CAARD 1985). S.K. Dey, the minister for community development (CD) in Nehru's cabinet and the architect of panchayati raj after independence, elevated the whole idea to a philosophical level and viewed it as an instrument which links the individual with the universe. Within the sphere of national democracy he visualised an organic and intimate relationship between the Gram Sabha and the Lok Sabha (Dey 1961: 87).

A Promising Start

By 1959 all the states had passed panchayat acts, and by the mid-1960s panchayats had reached all parts of the country. There was enthusiasm in rural India and a feeling gripped the people that they had a say in affairs affecting their daily lives. Those were the promising days of panchayati raj institutions in India. It is worthwhile looking into some of the official reports on panchayati raj to get a picture of the positive aspects of the system. A report of the ministry of community development had stated in 1964-65 that younger and better leadership was emerging through the panchayati raj institutions and there was a fairly high degree of satisfaction among the people with their working. L.P. Shukla (1964) underscored the significance of this new leadership. According to him, the establishment of the panchayati raj institutions gave a boost to the emergence of local leadership by creating new seats of power to be filled by the competitive mechanism of democratic elections. This enabled a large number of people to acquire leadership at the local levels because, in the earlier traditional, socio-political set up they had no access to the political or administrative organs (1964: 10). Another perceptive writer, R.V. Jathar, had noted:

> If the policy of the government in giving impetus to the Panchayati Raj movement is implemented faithfully and fully, it will surely bring about the political, social and economic revolution which will not only strengthen the democratic character of our society, but will also prove a perennial source of... energetic, honest and competent leaders with potentialities to change the entire face of the country and guide the destinies of the people most efficiently and effectively (1964: 1).

This was written in 1964 after looking closely at the working of panchayati raj institutions in India. In yet another case, a study team appointed by the Association of Voluntary Agencies for Rural Development (AVARD) in 1962 evaluated panchayati raj in Rajasthan a year after the programme was launched:

> It was reported that the people felt that they had sufficient powers to enable them to mould their future....They are fully conscious of the fact that such privileges and favours which were formerly under the control of the B.D.O [block development officer] are now under their control. In this sense full advantage of democratic decentralisation has been secured (1962: 8-9).

The report then proceeded to say that the conferring of power on people's representatives had improved the attendance of teachers in primary schools, while block administration had become more responsive, people voiced their grievance before the *pradhans* (the chairpersons of local self-government institutions) and got relief through them, and above all petty corruption, both among the subordinate staff as well as among the newly elected leaders, had declined; the former because the block staff had come under the Panchayat Samiti and the latter because the public reputation of the pradhans was crucial for them to get re-elected. For B. Maheswari (1963), panchayati raj institutions fulfilled all the functions of a local government and acted as the "primary schools of democracy." Due to the interest generated by the panchayati raj institutions in the states, several states set up committees to assess the working of the panchayati raj institutions and to recommend measures for improvement.[2]

The Downhill Slide

Nevertheless the panchayati raj system was moving downhill. In Abhijit Datta's (1985: 562) view, panchayati raj institutions had become only a "living caricature of local government." In an editorial comment, Thomas Matthai despaired that the village panchayat had been reduced to "a focus of frustration. The Gram Sabha is something of a joke" (*Democratic World,* 22 January 1978). Of course, its resources were meagre. That could have been set right if there had been the political will. The critical problem was the domination of panchayati raj institutions by the economically and socially privileged classes. This is essentially a socio-political problem and could have been tackled to a great extent by holding elections at regular intervals. The resulting political education of communities, oppressed for ages, would have certainly changed the scenario.

An example comes from the elections to the Tamil Nadu local bodies held after a lapse of sixteen years in 1986. It is interesting to note the social consequences these generated. For instance, in Kamudhi Town Panchayat in Ramanathapuram District, the Muslims and the Nadar community had been arch enemies for the previous fifty to sixty years. Over the past thirty years they had opposed each other in the elections to the local bodies but this time, without precedent, they got together and fielded a common candidate and got him elected. If regular elections are held, permutations and combinations change, traditional rivalries disappear and issue-oriented groupings emerge. In this process, simple mechanical solidarity gives way to more organic solidarity where individual freedom of opinion and group decisions emerge. In another case, a Muslim defied the local Muslim *Jamaath* (organisation), contested the poll and secured 276 votes out of the four hundred votes in the three Muslim wards. Multiple such examples can be found all over the country. It is precisely this process that had been arrested for years by state governments, by either frequently postponing or not holding the elections at all. The committee set up by the national Planning Commission, with G.V.K. Rao as chairman, had stated in its report:

> Apart from inadequate resources, elections to these bodies have not been held regularly. In fact, elections have become overdue for one or more tiers of the Panchayati Raj Institutions in eleven States, and in eight States even elections to Gram Panchayats are overdue. Elections have been put off on one pretext or another...and the term of the existing bodies have been extended or the bodies have been superseded (CAARD 1985: 41).

Evidence suggests that there was a deliberate plan by the bureaucracy, the local vested interests and their elected representatives in the state legislatures and in the parliament to cripple and eventually discard panchayati raj, because its ascendancy was feared.

The roots of this hidden agenda could be traced to 1960 when the government launched an intensive agricultural district programme (IADP), by-passing the community development programmes. The Jayaprakash Narayan committee of 1960 detected double-thinking and contradictory positions developing within the government in the creation of an independent intensive agricultural district programme. The committee said that after having accepted panchayati raj as the agency responsible for planning and executing of plans, "there is no longer any valid reason for the continuing individual allocations subject-wise even to serve as a guide" (Jain et al. 1985: 39). Evidently, the CD ministry was uneasy with the launching of the intensive agricultural district programme. But soon schemes like the Small Farmers Development Agency (SFDA), the Drought Prone Areas Programme (DPAP) or the Intensive Tribal Development Programme (ITDP) were also introduced though outside the purview of the elected zilla parishads. Plan allocations to the latter's jurisdiction were tapered off.

In 1966-67 the ministry of community development was reduced to the status of a department and brought under the ministry of food and agriculture. Coupled with this the government launched a few schemes of integrated district plans in twenty-eight districts of twelve states and abandoned two instruments for appraisal, that is, the annual development conference and the annual evaluation by the programme evaluation organisation. "This lent support to the view that not only the CD ministry but the CD project itself had been downgraded" (Jain et al. 1985: 40). In 1971, the very title, "Community Development," was dropped and replaced by "Rural Development." "This was not just a cosmetic change. It marked the end of both the 'community' and 'panchayats' as agents of change and agencies of development," observes L.C. Jain (et al. 1985: 44). In the words of the Asoka Mehta committee "The essential idea that all developmental activities should flow only through the block-level organisation lost ground, though the Panchayat Samiti as a key unit of decentralisation was, in most cases, coterminous with the block" (1978: 4). It may be emphasized here that all the development programmes were bureaucracy-centred with hardly any participation of the people.

Thus the bureaucracy gained the upper hand in a grand alliance with the state and central-level political elite. The role of the bureaucracy in bringing down panchayati raj to its present plight is brought out sharply by the Asoka Mehta committee:

> [The] bureaucracy had probably its own role in dissociating the PRIs from the development process. Several factors seem to have conditioned their perception. The system of line hierarchy would find favour with them as an organisational principle. The officers would feel that they are primarily accountable for results and financial proprieties to the state government. The

officials knew no better than to trust their non-fraternity. They would, on the one hand, therefore be averse to the PRIs being entrusted with additional functions and on the other would not easily get adjusted to working under the supervision of elected representatives (1978: 5-6).

This was not just a phenomenon typical to independent India. Whatever semblance of local self-government existed in the British period in India was destroyed by officialdom. For example, the report of the Village Panchayat Committee of the All-India Congress Committee (AICC), in analysing the main reasons for the disintegration of village panchayats, had stated that, "the inordinate greed of the East India Company caused slow but steady disintegration of these Village Panchayats....The excessive *centralisation of the executive and judicial powers in the hands of the Government officials deprived the village functionaries of their age long powers and influence"* (AICC 1954: 10-11) (emphasis added).

We have noted that Lord Ripon made an earnest effort to introduce local self-government, but it failed. Why? The Indian Statutory Commission of 1929 had stated that whatever might have been the intentions of Lord Ripon, his reforms in the sphere of local self-government were not free from *official control* and "no real attempt was made to inaugurate a system amenable to the will of the local inhabitants" (Shukla 1964)

Why did the political elite play to the tune of the bureaucracy? The reason is not far to seek. After all, politicians would not like to see the erosion of their power by a breed of new, local leadership. Thus it is legitimate to conclude that a combination of the bureaucracy, commercial interests, the professional middle class, the police and the political elite "ganged up" against democratic decentralisation. A thesis was developed and popularised that a centralised bureaucracy can benefit the rural poor better than local elected "vested interests." The result? "We have ended up creating an impregnable alliance of urban officialdom and the rural rich, and have excluded the rural poor from it" (Rajni Kothari, in his foreword to Jain et al. 1985)

Causes of Failure

Gandhiji's vision of *gram swaraj* (village republics) was first shattered when in their wisdom our constitution-makers put panchayati raj in the directive principles of the constitution, merely saying that the state shall take steps to organise village panchayats with powers to function as units of self-government. This put little obligation on anyone to implement the ideas expounded by Gandhiji on village swaraj in the *Harijan* (July 1942). He had spoken of a village republic in which the government would be annually elected by adult villagers and which would have the authority and jurisdiction in the fields of legislation, judiciary and executive decision making without interference from the state government. Gandhiji saw panchayats as a perfect democracy based upon individual freedom.

India's development in the early fifties was planned without taking cognizance of Gandhiji's idea of gram swaraj. It did not take long to realise the folly of this line of approach. The Community Development project, inaugurated in 1952 and modelled after the experiments at Marthandam, Shantiniketan, Baroda, Etawa and Nilokheri, soon found itself in a blind alley in the absence of effective instruments for people's participation.

The Balwantrai Mehta study team's report (1957) was a critical turning point. The report affirmed that community development can be real only when the community exercises the necessary powers through its chosen representatives and maintains a constant and intelligent vigilance on local administration. Therefore, it recommended the establishment of statutory elective local bodies. This belated realisation paved the way for the first generation panchayati raj.

On 2 October 1959 when Jawaharlal Nehru had inaugurated panchayati raj at a national rally in Naguar in Rajasthan, the people had rejoiced because there were signs of Gandhiji's dream coming true at last. The period between 1959 and 1964 can be described as the golden period of the first generation panchayati raj institutions. Younger and better leadership had begun to emerge through the competitive mechanism of democratic elections, which enabled a large number of people to acquire leadership at the local level.

By the mid-sixties panchayats had emerged in most parts of the country. There were over 217,300 village panchayats, covering over 96 percent of the 579,000 inhabited villages and 92 percent of the rural population. On an average, a panchayat covered a population of about 2,400, in two to three villages.

The rejoicing of the people was short-lived. After Nehru's death, political leaders were determined to end the threat to their leadership from the village, mandal or district leadership. They paid only lip service to local self-government. The bureaucracy, in alliance with local powers, state and central-level politicians, began to discredit the new system by highlighting its shortcomings. It saw in these local bodies the domination of the upper or dominant castes, corruption and total ineptitude. Had Nehru been around, he would have made his characteristic response: "Let village authorities function and let them make a million mistakes." The district, mandal and village bodies were starved of funds. Thus village panchayats were reduced to a focus of frustration, and *gram sabhas* (village assemblies) became a joke. Elections were either not held or were frequently postponed. In most cases these bodies were superseded.

I consider panchayati raj of the Nehruvian era as the first generation because in this period the panchayati raj institutions were conceived as local bodies meant to ensure peoples participation in development. This phase started on 2 October 1959 (when Jawaharlal Nehru inaugurated panchayati raj) and the decline began with Nehru's disappearance from the scene in 1964. For about thirteen years after that, from 1964 to 1977, panchayati raj remained the whipping boy of all those who wanted to discredit the decentralisation of power.

Notes

1. The Team for the Study of Community Projects and National Extension Service (known as the Balwantrai Mehta committee) was constituted by the committee on plan projects in 1957. The recommendations of the committee favouring democratic decentralisation through setting up of panchayati raj institutions accelerated the pace of constituting PRIs in all states through panchayat acts.

2. The states and committees were:

Andhra Pradesh	Purushottam Pai Committee, 1964
	Ramachandra Reddy Committee, 1965
	Narasimhan Committee, 1972
Karnataka	Basappa Committee, 1963
Maharashtra	Naik Committee, 1961
	Bongiwar Committee, 1963
Rajasthan	Mathur Committee, 1963
	Sadiq Ali Committee, 1963
	G.L. Vyas Committee, 1973
Uttar Pradesh	Govind Sahai Committee, 1959
	Ram Murti Committee, 1965 (Jain et al. 1985: 40).

3

The Second Generation

Integrating the Four Pillar State

The appointment of the Asoka Mehta committee in 1977 marked a turning point in the concepts and practice of panchayati raj, and the second generation can be said to have started when the West Bengal government took the initiative in 1978 to give a new life to its panchayats on the lines of the Asoka Mehta committee recommendations. The committee report is essentially a seminal document to make panchayats "an organic, integral part of our democratic process."

The vital difference between the first and second generation of panchayats is the shift in emphasis from development *per se* to local government in its full meaning. The Balwantrai Mehta committee made development central to the panchayat system, while the attempt in West Bengal, Karnataka, Andhra Pradesh, and later on Jammu and Kashmir, has been to make panchayats into genuine political institutions and thus the focal point of self-government with all its ramifications, a microcosm of the state itself.

The state governments could not establish full-fledged panchayati raj without adequate constitutional safeguards. In all the states where devolution of power to the villages was attempted the concentration of power at the centre worked as an impediment. For instance, in 1985, Abdul Nazir Sab, the minister for panchayati raj in Karnataka under the Janata government had stated:

> Soon we realised that within the limitations imposed by the Constitution, the ideology of a "Four Pillar State"–village, district, state and centre–could not be implemented *in toto* by the state government....Without a constitutional amendment guaranteeing

> the "Four Pillar State," our efforts may not be as fruitful as we desire. In my opinion this is the major question the intellectuals of this country must ponder over. They must create a public debate on the necessity of a constitutional amendment (Nazir Sab 1986).

The underlying issue is that any move to revitalise the local bodies and introduce a new system of governance below the state level can be effective only if it is accompanied by genuine federalism, in theory and practice, at the national level. In its absence, such measures are just form without content. This chapter attempts to describe some of the important features of the second generation panchayati raj and underline some significant pointers for the future. The most important thrust of the second phase was that the panchayat emerged from a development organisation at the local level into a political institution. The emphasis shifted from the bureaucracy to the political elements. This was a welcome trend.

West Bengal, Karnataka, Andhra Pradesh and Jammu and Kashmir either revised their existing panchayat acts or passed new acts, in theory accepting the Asoka Mehta committee report. These states adapted the recommendations to suit their conditions and learnt from each other's experience in bringing forth new legislations or amendments to the prevailing acts. For instance, in 1983 Karnataka followed the West Bengal experience begun in 1978, and soon Andhra Pradesh also opened a new chapter, taking the cue from Karnataka and West Bengal.

Official Involvement of Political Parties

In West Bengal, the local elections of 4 June 1978 witnessed the official participation of political parties for the first time in India. Although there was no legal bar on the participation of non-party candidates, according to a study by the National Institute of Rural Development (NIRD), the prevailing political climate and administrative arrangements had the effect of discouraging such participation.

There was considerable opposition to the involvement of political parties in local elections but the Communist Party of India-Marxist (CPI-M) and its allies preferred the official recognition of parties in the panchayats elections. They believed that the direct involvement of political parties in the panchayat institutions would make its leadership more disciplined and responsible in managing these institutions of rural democracy and could put an end to the age-old tradition of rural coteries reaping the benefits for narrow, sectarian and caste interests.

Two noteworthy features of these elections, as brought out by the NIRD study, were that there was a high degree of political perception among the rural voters with no influence of caste in the socio-economic matrix, and for the first time there emerged a new, youthful, literate, rural leadership in West Bengal. The political background for the above welcome change was to be attributed to the promises made by the Left Front government for substantial devolution of powers and resources to the local bodies, and the large-scale enthusiasm created among the villagers due to the participation of political parties.

In Karnataka, the local bodies elections of January 1987 were held on party lines for the first time. Karnataka also witnessed opposition to elections being held on party lines. But the Janata party stood its ground by asking: If political parties are indispensable for parliamentary democracy, is it not important that they must take root in the villages through the elections to the village bodies which are the nurseries of democracy?

During the election campaign the discussions and debates in village tea shops and market places were elevated to the level of political ideologies, the assessment of balance sheets of political parties and the track record of political leaders.

There is a general tendency to think that the ideal situation is to have consensus candidates in panchayats but it is not difficult to see that in villages the coercive power of traditional caste alignments, bullies and money makes it possible for a person to keep getting elected as a consensus member for years altogether. When people align on the basis of the policies and programmes of political parties, these types of problems are minimal.

When the Telugu Desam party (TDP) came to power in Andhra Pradesh it had no special emphasis on panchayati raj. But in its *Mahanadu* (great assembly) in May 1984 the party took the decision to bring in drastic changes in the redundant panchayati raj system formally established in Andhra Pradesh on I November 1959. Thus, the 1984 manifesto spoke about panchayati raj in unambiguous terms. It said that the Telugu Desam would work for a directly elected district administration which would form a third tier in the country's federal polity with proper constitutional backing so that people may have democratic self-government at the local level; not under the district bureaucracy, but over it.

The TDP took the Asoka Mehta committee recommendations of a two-tier system seriously but modified it slightly to include village panchayats also. Andhra Pradesh tried to evolve its own system of local self-government. The elections were held in March 1987 to the mandala praja parishads and zilla praja parishads on the basis of the 1986 act. These elections were held on party lines. They evoked great popular interest throughout the state, generating heated debates on political personalities, ideologies as well as people's issues and were popularly referred to as the "mini general elections."

It has now been clearly established that local bodies elections on party lines have made the villagers of these three states much more politically conscious, giving the elected panchayat bodies a political standing of their own. The local leadership has also become politically more responsible. Since the reputation of political parties depends on the integrity and performance of the local leaders, the accountability is much more in these cases.

Wider Participation

One of the indices of people's participation in local self-government is the large percentage of voter turn out in its elections. In all the three states mentioned above, whenever the elections to the panchayats were held there was a high percentage of polling, with women in many cases out-numbering men. Karnataka had been the first to reduce the voting age to eighteen in the country. Andhra Pradesh followed suit. This ensured youthful leadership and dynamism in the local bodies. Although the voting age was twenty-one in West Bengal (until it was lowered nationwide on 28 March 1989), young people were already on the forefront in these bodies. (According to a survey, 21 percent of the elected members in West Bengal were below thirty years.) The NIRD study of the 1978 elections has shown that about 51.1 percent of the panchayat members were in the age group of twenty-one to thirty-five. It is clear that in spite of the deference for age, people prefer younger candidates.

A related aspect of democratic participation in local elections, documented in Kirsten Westergaard's study of West Bengal (1986), was that a sizeable proportion of the elected representatives were from the lower castes and tribals and this representation was the first important step towards increasing the control over the panchayats on the part of the disadvantaged groups.

A step taken in this direction by Andhra Pradesh is the direct election of the Zilla Parishad chairman and Mandal Panchayat president. The fact that the entire electorate takes part in the election of their local bodies chairman/president at these two important levels is an indicator of the wider involvement of the people in the electoral process. However, there are serious questions about the type of people who can contest such elections because of the cost involved in such elections in large geographical areas. It may be recalled here that the Asoka Mehta committee had recommended only indirect elections for these posts.

Care for the Weaker Sections

It is now generally recognised that panchayats in the three states under review have inspired the rural people and created self-confidence among them. In a survey conducted in West Bengal it was found that 80 percent of the members came from among owner-cultivators, school teachers, the unemployed, landless labourers, crop-sharers and artisans. Over 71 percent of owner-cultivator members had land below five acres. Thus the majority came from the poorer sections in the villages. This is a revolutionary change which has come about through people getting political power as their right at the grassroots level.

In Karnataka the 1983 act reserved 25 percent of the seats for women and 20 percent for the Scheduled Castes and Scheduled Tribes (SCs/STs). This was the first time that such a progressive step had been taken in India. In Andhra Pradesh also reservations have been enhanced. Under the Andhra Pradesh Panchayat Samithis and Zilla Parishads Act, 1959, reservations were only for SCs and STs. The 1986 act provides for reservation of 20 percent seats for Backward Classes and 9 percent for women.

A major concern of Andhra Pradesh and Karnataka in the devolution of power was that the mandals should be small and convenient enough for all inhabitants of the area to avail of the services and participate in the administration. Therefore the mandal panchayats in Karnataka were based on the concept of the "growth centre" or "service centre" as envisaged in the Asoka Mehta committee report. The parallel in old Mysore were the *hoblies* (or the *firka* in north Karnataka).

In Andhra Pradesh the TDP government's promise was that it would take administration "to the doorstep of the poorest of the poor." The Mandala Praja Parishad (population: 30,000 to 60,000) will have a primary health centre, a junior college, a high school, a veterinary hospital, a telephone exchange, a commercial bank, a *grameena* (village) bank and a cooperative bank, a sub-treasury, a police station, a post office, a godown, market-yards, a vocational training centre and a credit cooperative society. N.T. Rama Rao, the then chief minister of Andhra Pradesh, had likened the mandala praja parishads to "mini capitals."

Earlier panchayat samithis were getting an annual per capita grant of ninety paise and the zilla parishads twenty paise. Now, mandala praja parishads will be getting a grant of five rupees and zilla praja parishads two rupees per capita. In Karnataka the government makes an annual grant at the rate of ten rupees per person residing within a mandal, 25 percent of which goes to the Zilla Parishad. Mandals have powers to levy taxes also.

In West Bengal, gram panchayats having a population numbering about ten thousand have become convenient units for local self-government. Moreover, the panchayat samitis which are at the block level have proved to be viable and convenient units. There are 3,242 gram panchayats and 324 panchayat samitis in West Bengal.

Primacy to Zilla Parishads

All the measures adopted by West Bengal, Karnataka and Andhra Pradesh, briefly surveyed above, converge to a district government approach for the time being as the second generation panchayats seem to be giving more weight to the zilla parishads. For instance, in West Bengal the district magistrate has, in all cases, to assist the *sabhadhipati* (chairperson) of the Zilla Parishad. A convention has also been established in West Bengal which constrains the chairmen of the standing committees of the Zilla Parishad to meet regularly. This is a step forward in the direction of the cabinet system of functioning at the district level.

In Karnataka, the remuneration and perquisites, equivalent to those of a minister of state and deputy minister, which were being given to the Zilla Parishad *adhyakshas* (chairpersons) and *upadhyakshas* (vice-chairpersons) respectively, as well as the equivalent status attached to these posts, were other steps in this direction. There was a general consensus that the 1983 act of Karnataka was the most radical measure of decentralisation attempted so far and if properly implemented, would have converted Karnataka into something like a federation of districts. In Andhra Pradesh also the same status, remuneration and perquisites as in Karnataka were envisaged for the Zilla Parishad chairmen.

Emerging Tensions

The second phase of panchayati raj has disturbed the earlier "balance" between the role of officials and non-officials. Consequently, a process of trial and error, and of adjustment, will inevitably take place before the viewpoints of the official and the non-official side can be appreciated.

In Karnataka, serious questions on the bureaucracy throttling the panchayati raj initiative are being raised. Is the bureaucracy not hurt because the rural folk have become its masters under the new dispensation? Even in West Bengal it took some time before the new ethos began to be understood and a balance between the role of officials and non-officials could be achieved. Another question which attracts our attention is, will the inclusion of Members of Parliament (M.Ps), Members of the Legislative Assembly (M.L.As) and Members of the Legislative Council (M.L.Cs) in the local bodies help the growth of local leadership? It has been argued that their presence is meant to maintain the link between the Zilla Parishad and the policy-making bodies at the state and union government level.

The Asoka Mehta committee had, it may be recalled, suggested inclusion of nominees of only bigger municipalities, persons with a special interest in rural development and university teachers of the social sciences. It had excluded the M.Ps and M.L.As because they carry a lot of weight and their direct association with the Zilla Parishad would inhibit the emergence of local leadership.

In his dissent note to the Asoka Mehta committee report, E.M.S. Namboodiripad (the veteran CPI-M leader from Kerala), had said that even the presence of non-elected members might imply that the Zilla Parishad is a body concerned with development alone, thus relegating the political and democratic dimensions to the background.

Total freedom from the stranglehold of central and state level political leadership, non-elected members and officialdom is a prerequisite for the effective functioning of panchayati raj.

Political interference in the working of the heads of the panchayat bodies is the most dreaded aspect of present-day politics. This tends to be milder if the zilla parishads and mandals belong to the same party but severe if they belong to the opposition. One such issue, which has already come up, is the question of Mandal Panchayat reservations in the districts of Andhra Pradesh. Charges have been levelled in some districts that the reservations were decided not on the basis of the population of SCs and STs in a district, but on the basis of the political interests of the ruling party.

It is not desirable to vest the powers of supersession and dissolution directly in the government's hands. The central issue for a functioning democracy at the lowest level is that local level institutions should not exist at the sweet will and pleasure of the government in power. They should be autonomous and guided by the larger interests of the local community within the overall framework of national interest. This does not mean that there should not be any checks and balances. Such controls should exist but they should not be from above but built in horizontally, by the people themselves.

The Case of Jammu and Kashmir

It was encouraging that the state of Jammu and Kashmir provided a congenial setting for the success of measures like panchayati raj in 1988. This state has seen more radical social reform than many other states in the country. The economic backwardness of Kashmir tended to give a radical turn to its freedom movement. Although the National Conference (the regional party of the state) was predominantly middle class in composition, it found its main support among the peasantry and the artisans. This had driven the *Kashmiri* leadership to political and economic radicalism. The political programme of the National Conference was enshrined in the historic document, called *The New Kashmir,* which became the source of its policies and programmes.

One of the first steps taken by the first Jammu and Kashmir Assembly was to pass what became the most drastic piece of land reform legislation in India. Jawaharlal Nehru's response to this reform was expressed in the following words:

> I confess that I look with some envy on the speed and clarity with which they (Kashmir Government) have performed this task there, considering the enormous trouble we have had in the various States of India, the difficulties, the obstruction and the delays that we had to face, and so, I became a little envious when I saw this was done in Kashmir (Dhar 1964, 58: 14).

Given this social development, the Jammu and Kashmir Panchayati Raj Act, 1989, was meant to give a new thrust and direction to the state. This measure, intended to ensure people's participation in the affairs of the state, was also meant to pull the state out of the political turmoil in which, unfortunately, it has found itself of late. Moreover, panchayati raj is a sure way to protect *Kashmiri* culture and identity.

In 1958 the Jammu and Kashmir government had legislated the first village panchayat act. The act had received the assent of the *Sadar-i-Riyasat* (the head of the state) on 7 November 1958. The aim of this act was to make better provisions for the administration of village panchayats in Jammu and Kashmir.

Thirty years after the passing of the 1958 act, the Jammu and Kashmir government introduced another bill in the assembly on

21 April 1988 which was passed in March 1989. It may be noted that this new act envisages significant changes in the existing situation of the local self-government system in the state.

The salient features of the act are: a) reduction of the voting age from twenty-one to eighteen; b) holding elections within six months of supersession of a panchayat; c) direct election of the *sarpanch* (chairperson); d) reorganisation of the *panchayati adalats* (panchayat courts), consisting of three members, who are to be nominated by the government out of a panel recommended by the panchayat; e) empowering panchayats to plan and implement schemes for rural industrialisation, agriculture, animal husbandry, health and primary education (see Mathew 1990).

For effective participation of the rural population in the development programmes at the grassroots level the panchayat system will have three tiers: (i) *Halqa Panchayat* (group of village panchayats), which will meet once in a month and get its annual budget approved by the voters on the first working day of April every year; (ii) *Block Development Council*, which will have the responsibility of maintaining and supervising the inter-circle communication system. The block development councils will consist of all the sarpanches in a block, the M.L.As of the area (except minister), the chairman of any marketing committee or the notified area committee, along with the block development officer as the member secretary. The block development councils will get their grant from the government in proportion to the size of the council as directly elected by the people; (iii) *the district planning and development boards*, comprising the chairmen of all block development councils, the M.Ps and M.L.As from the districts, chairmen of two area committees and presidents of municipal councils, with district-level heads of all development departments as ex-officio members.

The Jammu and Kashmir act had generated considerable interest among the advocates of decentralisation. It had been hailed as an act "imaginatively conceived" which would infuse a new spirit of self-reliance and self-confidence in the people. The idea of a panchayati adalat was a novel and bold one.

The Jammu and Kashmir legislation assumed special significance because it came as a sequel to the efforts in states like West Bengal, Karnataka and Andhra Pradesh to take a fresh look at the working of the panchayati raj institutions as instruments of devolution of power to the people at the village level. In fact, the then minister for agriculture and rural development, Mohammad Shafi, had visited Karnataka State to study the working of the its panchayati raj.

While the 1958 act was limited in purpose essentially to provide for a suitable administrative structure for the village panchayats in the state, the 1989 act had envisaged significant changes at the district level and below. The thrust has been on the entire gamut of local self-government system and not on development functions alone. Therefore, the goal of the new legislation has been "to promote and develop panchayati raj in the State *as an instrument of vigorous local self-government* to secure the effective participation of the people in the decision-making process and for overseeing implementation of developmental programmes" [emphasis added] (Mathew 1990).

4

Decentralisation: Legislative and Constitutional Support

A nation may establish a free government but without municipal institutions it cannot have the spirit of liberty.

– Alexis de Tocqueville

It is well established that constitutional support and legislative measures are necessary for bringing about social change, but not a sufficient condition to achieve the goal. Our experience in the more than forty-six years since independence bears witness to this fact. This is true of democratic decentralisation also. Of course, one can argue that there was no constitutional support for local self-government below the state level and therefore we are in the state of affairs in which we find ourselves now. The other side of the same coin would be: we have constitutional guarantees and laws for many vexed problems we face in the society now but we are not in a position to say that we are better off because of these safeguards. Political will and people's political awareness are crucial for bringing about democratic decentralisation–local self-governments–below the state level, and only constitutional support or legislative measures can create the necessary conditions. A three-dimensional approach–political will, people's awareness, and building healthy conventions and traditions undergirded by constitutional and legislative measures–is a must for any far-reaching changes to be brought about in our society, and when one of these is weak the entire measure may remain in form without content.

Local Self-Government Acts before Independence

In 1882 the role of local administration was elevated by the introduction of the Ripon resolutions. Designed to make use of that intelligent class of public-spirited men whom it is not only bad policy but sheer waste of power to fail to utilise, the resolutions proposed the establishment of local rural boards, two-thirds of whose membership was composed of elected representatives. Therefore, as was mentioned earlier, the government resolution of 18 May 1882 during Lord Ripon's viceregal tenure was considered the Magna Carta of local democracy in India.

In Bengal these ideas were implemented through the Bengal Local Self-Government Act of 1885, which set up district boards, local boards at the sub-divisional levels and union committees for groups of villages. By 1925 eight provinces in British India had passed acts for the establishment of village panchayats. By 1948, twenty native states had village panchayat acts, the earliest being the Cochin Panchayats Regulations Act of 1919 and the last one, the Jaipur Village Panchayat Act, 1948. It is evident that these legislative measures, which covered a limited number of villages and had a limited number of functions, did not usher in local self-governments (that is, the "little republics").

We know that in spite of our history of panchayats and despite the commitment of the nationalist movement to village panchayats, the first draft of India's constitution did not find a place for democratic decentralisation below the state level. When Gandhiji learnt that the proposed constitution did not provide for panchayats, he had remarked that this was certainly an omission calling for immediate attention if India's independence was to reflect the people's voice.

First and Second Generation Panchayati Raj: State-level Acts

Following the report of the Balwantrai Mehta committee, almost all the states had passed legislations by 1959 to establish panchayats. But what happened after 1964 to these well-meaning measures, initiated by Jawaharlal Nehru and S.K.

Dey in the fifties, is too well known to recapitulate here. In fact, till 1977 the only national move to reinforce "statutory representative bodies" was the affirmation by the National Development Council of the basic principles of democratic decentralisation, leaving it to the states to work out the structures suitable to each state.

The non-functioning panchayati raj institutions brought disrepute to the entire concept and its practice. There was a growing realisation that it was the lack of constitutional support that had led to the sad state of affairs. For instance, Malcolm Adiseshiah, while commenting on Tamil Nadu not holding panchayat elections for fifteen years, noted that in these fifteen years the Tamil Nadu government had put forward twenty reasons for the postponement of local elections. It had announced elections twenty times and postponed them as many times. He remarked:

> I must say that this is a situation not peculiar to Tamil Nadu. It exists in most states. There are no elections to local bodies. As a result of this, corruption becomes rampant in all programmes affecting the people. I would like to ask the question: Why is it that we cannot have a constitutional amendment which will make it obligatory for local elections to be held on time? (Adiseshiah 1986: 25).

Adiseshiah felt that all the twenty reasons used to postpone the Tamil Nadu local elections could also be used for withholding elections to the Lok Sabha and the state assemblies. He continued, "Here I add my plea that we should earnestly work for a constitutional amendment to panchayati raj elections on the same footing as the Lok Sabha and State Assembly elections" (1986: 25).

In 1977 the Asoka Mehta committee had emphasized the need for a constitutional amendment. The acts, or amendments to the earlier acts (e.g., the West Bengal Panchayat Act of 1973 on which the West Bengal Left Front government made fifteen amendments from 1978 till 1988), which were passed following the Asoka Mehta committee recommendations in West Bengal, Karnataka, Andhra Pradesh, Jammu and Kashmir and Kerala, formed the basis for the second generation panchayati raj. Since these acts gave more powers to the local bodies and as their orientation was more political than developmental, they evoked widespread enthusiasm both in their implementation as well as their working. The West Bengal pattern was considered a success story. The single major reason for the 1985 victory of the Janata party in Karnataka was attributed to the party's commitment to implement the "power to the people" promise. Abdul Nazir Sab, at the time the minister for panchayati raj and rural development, had said that he had witnessed a real awakening in the people when they realised that they could share power at the lower level.

But Nazir Sab had made another significant observation also. According to him, "the Four Pillar State"–the village, district, state and centre–in India had been the dream of the Father of the Nation (Mahatma Gandhi) but when Karnataka set out to implement this in earnest, it was realised that within the limitations imposed by the constitution, this ideology could not be implemented by a state government on its own. He was emphatic, given his experience, that the intentions to bring about radical structural changes in the governance of a state may be laudable but without a constitutional amendment these intentions and efforts may not be as fruitful as one desires. At a seminar organised by the Institute of Social Sciences in Delhi in 1985 Nazir Sab had pleaded with intellectuals to ponder over this question and to create a public debate on the necessity of a constitutional amendment.

Demands for Constitutional Support

With the remarkable enthusiasm among the ordinary people in West Bengal and Karnataka on the implementation of panchayati raj, the moves to incorporate constitutional provisions for panchayati raj strengthened. Four dominant views regarding the discussions that took place during that period could be identified:

1. The constitutional changes to guarantee elections to local bodies at the expiry of their term is a sufficient condition for bringing life into the local bodies.

2. The constitutional guarantee of elections is not a sufficient condition but only a necessary condition. What is really needed is a "quantum jump" in political democracy providing for a three or four-tier government, that is, the centre, state, district and village governments.
3. Local self-governments must be strengthened, but not through rigid and uniform constitutional provisions. Freedom at the state and regional levels for experimenting and evolving suitable systems is a must.
4. A "marriage" of district government and panchayati raj is possible. The concept of people's participation must be considered as an ideological commitment and therefore what are needed are legislative and structural measures to give legitimacy to people's participation.

By the end of 1988 a sub-committee of the consultative committee of parliament under the chairmanship of an M.P., P.K. Thungon, made recommendations for strengthening the panchayati raj system. One of its important recommendations was that panchayati raj bodies should be constitutionally recognised.

It was against this backdrop that the Constitution (64th Amendment) Bill was drafted and introduced in parliament on 15 May 1989. By and large it was modelled on the bill (drafted by L. M. Singhvi) appended to the Asoka Mehta committee report of 1978. Although the 1989 bill in itself was a welcome step, there was serious opposition to it on two basic grounds and due to its political overtones. These were: a) the bill overlooked the state and was seen as an instrument of the centre to deal directly with the panchayati raj institutions; and, b) that it was imposing a uniform pattern throughout the country instead of permitting individual states to legislate the details, keeping in mind the local circumstances.

The National Front government introduced the 74th Amendment Bill (a combined bill on panchayats and municipalities) in 1990 during its short tenure in office but it was never taken up for discussion.

Centre's Move for Decentralisation?

There are some who express serious doubts about the wisdom of a constitutional amendment for making panchayati raj institutions functional and effective. Nirmal Mukarji (former Cabinet Secretary) has made certain observations[1] in this regard, which may be summed up as follows:

1. One of the arguments in favour of a constitutional amendment is that panchayati raj institutions need to achieve the requisite status as well as assurance of continuous functioning. One wonders whether status really flows out of a constitutional provision by itself. If the constitutional amendment bill were to be passed, would it really make a difference, given the absence of regular elections to panchayats and the prolonged supersessions? In West Bengal and Karnataka the panchayati raj experiment had proved to be a success even without any constitutional amendment of the kind that was being talked about.
2. Given the culture of violence and the feudal relations in the rural areas, would states like Bihar and Uttar Pradesh be able to pass the requisite statutes in line with whatever was stated in the constitution? Then again, even if the statutes are passed, given the harsh realities of these states, would these statutes be implemented in letter and spirit or would they remain laws on paper only?
3. Was there any requisite sanction in the bill for enforcing the provisions? If panchayati raj were to be enforced, would this be in tune with the spirit of democracy? Basically, the key question was whether a constitutional provision can by itself be an adequate substitute for political will.
4. The plain fact was that the political will appeared to be missing in the states ruled by those parties which were the loudest in their support for the bill. These parties kept introducing bills to amend the constitution. It seemed to salve their consciences. What prevented them from putting through, in the states which were under their control, that which they wanted to provide in the constitution? Such bills lacked credibility and could as well remain ineffective if enacted.

5. Is implementing decentralisation below the state level through the most centralising of all conceivable instruments–a constitutional amendment–desirable? A constitutional amendment is a drastic and irreversible instrument of a central government. Each of the many constitutional amendments effected had been at the intervention of the then central government. No amendment bill can possibly get through without the support of the centre. Can we ram decentralisation downwards to the states simply by a constitutional fiat from Delhi? Should not the whole question of decentralisation below the state level be left entirely to the states? Moreover, a constitutional amendment at the centre could well mean thrusting a uniform prescription on states which are widely disparate in administrative culture, in historical background and in demographic size.

Need for Constitutional and Legislative Support

In spite of Nirmal Mukarji's persuasive arguments, it is not difficult to see, in retrospect, that a constitutional amendment was a must for panchayati raj institutions. In essence, his argument was that there are certain prerequisites for local bodies to function as local self-government. It may be noted that in spite of the best legislation, vested interests always find loopholes to evade the law. Land reforms and a host of other social legislations are cases in point. Social scientists have gone into various aspects of the issue as to why in some states these legislations have achieved a measure of success, while other states have a dismal record.

Even in matters which have received constitutional support, things are not moving in the correct direction. Take the case of states coming under president's rule through the arbitrary dismissal of duly elected governments or the postponement of elections to suit the convenience of a particular party (in most cases, the party in power), or the allegations that constitutional authorities like the Election Commission are trying to postpone elections in some constituencies or in some particular states? All these come within the same mould.

We could argue that the political awareness of the people is a sufficient antidote to check the misuse of constitutional provisions. Kerala and Karnataka are two states which have a high level of political participation and awareness. But these two very states have seen the emasculation of local bodies by the new Congress(I) governments, which came to power after the Left Democratic Front and Janata governments, which had ruled these two states respectively and which had laid the foundations for sound decentralised governance there.

We now have great expectations from the democratic decentralisation that has taken place in West Bengal. It may be noted that West Bengal has achieved this level under the uninterrupted rule of one political party. Suppose a change takes place in West Bengal and a party which does not take decentralisation as an article of faith comes to power? It could be that the local self-government institutions, assiduously built over the years, could come under severe strain, as had happened in the case of Karnataka and Kerala. It is well known that the Congress(I) government in Andhra Pradesh was uncomfortable with the Andhra Pradesh mandala praja parishads, zilla praja parishads and zilla abhivrudhi sameeksha mandals established by the Telugu Desam party and plans were made to destroy the mandal system. Of course, with the constitutional amendment the situation may change a wee bit.

Along with the change of political managers another factor to be taken serious note of is the attitude of the bureaucracy. This is also a much debated topic and the success or failure of constitutional provisions/legislations depends a lot on the bureaucracy. It is a welcome fact that their attitude has been changing over the years towards people's representatives below the state level. After all, there is no other option for them than to recognise the sovereignty of the people and respect their representatives.

There is no substitute for healthy conventions and traditions in democratic politics and we must recognise them as the backbone of our society and polity. We have to build healthy, desirable conventions and if that happens it will be extremely difficult for any one, singly or collectively, to subvert them. The county and city local government institutions below the state level in the U.S.A. have had a satisfactory existence for so many decades and one of the reasons cited for this are the traditions of democracy that they have preserved with extreme care. In India, however, from independence onwards, violations of conventions have been of a very high magnitude. In such a context, what is the sanctity of constitutional amendments or legislations alone?

To conclude, let me quote from a recent study of West Bengal's panchayati raj and decentralisation process, conducted by Neil Webster. Speaking about the continuing inequalities in village life, Webster notes:

> Decentralisation and the transfer of power and resources to the panchayats is not enough to remove these problems as the socio-economic structures that oppose any attempt to democratise a class-based system run very deep. In 1977 as the Left Front set about revitalising the panchayats, it saw it in terms of a political movement for which the poorer peasantry and agricultural labourers had to be mobilised. Its successful future would seem to rely on its retaining that political dynamic (1990: 147).

I am afraid the Congress(I) lacks this political dynamics and without it the constitutional amendment will only be a paper tiger.

Note

1. Nirmal Mukarji had made these observations on 25 September 1991, in a panel discussion organised by the Institute of Social Sciences in New Delhi to discuss the Constitution (Seventy-second Amendment) Bill. The other panelists included L. C. Jain and Arun Ghosh, both former members of the Planning Commission. (For the proceedings of the panel discussion see, ISS 1991.)

5

From Legislation to Movement

The passing of the Constitution (Seventy-second Amendment) Bill on 22 December 1992 by parliament to incorporate the panchayats in Part IX of the constitution has set right a serious lapse in our constitution.[1] The argument for a constitutional amendment had gathered momentum in the second half of the eighties. There were two reasons for this. First, the concentration of power in Delhi had reached a flash point, threatening to break the very foundations of our polity. Therefore, the slogan, "power to the people" raised the demand for decentralised structures down to the village level. Second, the popularity of governments which had implemented successful panchayats in West Bengal and Karnataka had sent signals that this was an effective instrument to win the hearts of the rural masses. The concrete measures taken in 1989 to give constitutional sanction to panchayats have now borne fruit, after about four years of tortuous journey.

Legislative Initiatives

The 64th Amendment Bill, passed by the Lok Sabha but defeated in the Rajya Sabha in October 1989, as well as the 74th Amendment Bill introduced in parliament on 7 September 1990 by the National Front government have been discussed profusely in political circles. The bill, when it was introduced again in 1991, as well as the report of the Joint Committee of Parliament on this bill, had attracted widespread attention. However, some aspects of the bill as passed on 22-23 December 1992 by the Lok Sabha and the Rajya Sabha respectively require our attention.[2]

The major flaw of the new act of December 1992 is that it has adopted a uniform three-tier system below the state level. Even in bigger states like Karnataka, Tamil Nadu and Assam, which had three-tiers, there were structural differences in the system of panchayats. Haryana, Manipur, Kerala, Sikkim and the union territory of Lakshadweep had only two-tiers. Goa, Jammu and Kashmir, Tripura and several other union territories had only one-tier. It would have been better to leave the states to decide the number of tiers they required in line with their specific socio-historical milieu. It appears artificial to create a fixed number of tiers irrespective of a states' history and tradition. The AIADMK (All-India Anna Dravida Munnetra Kazhagam) and the DMK (Dravida Munnetra Kazhagam) members had spoken vehemently against this three-tier uniformity on the basis of their experience in Tamil Nadu but their amendments were not supported by others, and hence theirs remained a lone voice. Even the dissenting voice of the Marxists, who had spoken against uniformity in legislation, finally gave in. The only concession given was that at the intermediate level, panchayats need not be constituted in states with a population of less than two million. It seems that if the two-tier model were to be adopted, or the states which had found this model more suitable, had been left to themselves, it would have been akin to the Socialist-Janata supported concept of a four pillar state. Perhaps this was too much for the Congress(I) to concede.

The above-mentioned constitution amendment bill, when introduced, had provided for direct elections to the post of chairman at the village and intermediary levels. At the district level, it was left to the legislatures to decide. The Joint Committee of Parliament went into this question, but advocated direct elections only at the village level. The Marxist members of the joint committee had objected to direct elections at any level. But in order to achieve a consensus the Marxists had suggested that the issue of the election of the chairperson at the village level may be left to the state legislatures. In the end, the stand of the Left prevailed. Without arguing about the plus and minuses of indirect or direct elections, it may be said that direct elections to the post of chairpersons are more in consonance with the presidential form of government and indirect elections in conformity with the cabinet system of government, the latter being the one adopted in India.

Another lacuna in the bill was the contradictory and inconsistent approach to the idea that panchayats are institutions of self-government. The bill had rightly defined the panchayat as an institution of self-government but later, in defining the functions of this institution, had narrowed them down to developmental functions, as in Article 243 G(a) and (b). Without policing (law and order) as a function at each level, no institution of self-government is worth the name. When the 1983 act of Karnataka was discussed at a meeting of the Institute of Social Sciences, I remember Swami Agnivesh (the noted social activist) asking Nazir Sab, the prime mover of that historic bill, "Who will wield the *lathi* (a heavy stick used as an arm) in villages? Whose orders will the police take to use force?" Nazir Sab's answer was, "It is our intention that the police should come under the control of the zilla parishads. But we cannot do all these things simultaneously. We will do it step-by-step when the district government is constituted" (Nazir Sab 1986: 58).

Now that the "district government" idea has come into vogue, this crucial point is sadly missing. Nirmal Mukarji (a strong advocate of panchayats), given his vast experience in administration, had termed this dilution of the concept of institutions of self-government as "flawed thinking and drafting."

Resistance to Local Government

Wherever panchayats have not taken root or wherever they have been uprooted after brief spells of success, it has been observed that the Members of Parliament and state legislatures have been not too friendly to these institutions. Not only have these persons been indifferent to local governments, but at times they have also been hostile to these bodies. No one likes to see another centre of power emerging as a challenge, nor does one like to see ones existing powers being diluted. So much so, I am of the view that had it not been for the fact that the state legislatures were created along with the parliament, our respected M.Ps would not have allowed even the state legislatures to come up, once they had tasted power in the initial years. They would have justified their attitude with the argument that since they could look after the interests of all those whom they represented, why have another tier similar to that of the state, with all its nuisance value? In fact, the arguments of the M.L.As and M.Ps have been in the same vein and against the strengthening or revitalising of panchayats. Perhaps this is the reason why, in an attempt to assuage their feelings and to pre-empt any mischief from them, the M.Ps and M.L.As have been given membership and voting rights in the panchayats in the statutes now passed. This, to my mind, will undermine the panchayats which we are now aiming to strengthen. E.M.S. Namboodiripad's observations, incorporated in the Asoka Mehta committee report, are worth recalling here. Namboodiripad was in favour of purely elected bodies at all levels of panchayati raj. Having co-opted members, he believed, was a hangover of the idea that panchayati raj institutions are concerned with development alone and are not the elected organs of administration at the appropriate level.

With the states being asked to give more powers and departments to panchayats, the oft-repeated and vexed question the centre may frequently confront is: When will it devolve more powers to the states? This question will have to be answered, if not today, then in the near future.

If we had waited for a perfect legislative measure it would have been an utopia. What we have now got (in the form of the seventy-third constitutional amendment) is a major step forward. The provisions with regard to regular elections, reservation of one-third seats for women, reservation for SCs and STs (including for the office of the chairpersons), constitution of a finance commission, powers to raise resources, are welcome features of this long awaited measure to realise local self-government.

Amendments are always possible, even after the act is implemented. The urgent and immediate task had been to get the ratification of the minimum thirteen state assemblies (which was achieved by April 1993) so that the bill could receive the president's assent.

Any number of constitutional amendments will not usher in meaningful devolution of power or vibrant panchayats. Only strong political will can usher in real panchayati raj. For that, a movement is necessary. In the last few years state governments have realised that panchayats are the *sine qua non* for people's participation in development and for their prosperity. Panchayat success stories have been talked about across the country.

Ordinary people also know them. The demand for panchayats has been gathering the momentum of a people's movement.

The constitutional status accorded to panchayats, which have been the whipping boy of the bureaucrats, M.L.As, M.Ps and the rural and urban elites, will become a success story only if it is supported by a strong people's movement to give it the necessary momentum.

Notes

1. This became the Constitution (Seventy-third Amendment) Act, 1992.
2. The Constitution (64th Amendment) Bill was introduced in the Lok Sabha (lower house) on 15 May 1989. It secured two-thirds of the votes in the Lok Sabha but was defeated in the Rajya Sabha (upper house) on 15 October 1989. Making this an issue, the Congress(I) dissolved the Lok Sabha and went to polls in November 1989. Following the elections, the National Front came to power with V.P. Singh as prime minister and introduced the Constitution (74th Amendment) Bill in the Lok Sabha on 7 September 1990, for both panchayats and municipalities. It was not even taken up for discussion as the government went out of power on 9 November 1990. Next, the Congress government under Narasimha Rao introduced the bill in September 1991. It was referred to a Joint Select Committee of parliament. The Lok Sabha passed the bill on 22 December 1992 while the Rajya Sabha passed it the following day. Following the ratification by more than half the state assemblies, the president gave his assent on 20 April 1993. The act was brought into force by a government notification on 24 April 1993 as the Constitution (Seventy-third Amendment) Act, 1992.

Part Two

The Experience of Karnataka

6

The Beginnings

In 1956 when Karnataka (then called Mysore) came into being the state had inherited different local self-government laws. The Karnataka Village Panchayats and Local Boards Act, 1959, was only an attempt at uniform legislation, with no effort having been made to confer real powers and resources to the panchayati raj institutions. A committee was constituted, with Kondaji Basappa as its chairman, to recommend a suitable structure for the state. The committee submitted its report in 1963 and a bill was introduced in 1964 to establish a three-tier structure of local self-government. Ramakrishna Hegde, who was then the minister for rural development, headed the select committee which recommended enhanced powers to the panchayati raj institutions. Neither the ruling party in the state nor the government was interested in such radical steps and as a result nothing happened in this direction. The state had to wait till 1983 until a new government, with the political will for genuine democratic decentralisation, came to power.

The Karnataka Zilla Parishads, Taluk Panchayat Samitis, Mandal Panchayats and Nyaya Panchayats Bill was introduced in the state legislature in August 1983. Since the ruling Janata party did not have an absolute majority on its own, it had to accept certain compromises. One such compromise was the continuation of the taluk panchayat samitis (replacing the existing taluk development boards) though they were to have no executive functions of their own but would only have been endowed with powers of supervision, review and coordination, acting as agents of the Zilla Parishad and coordinating on its behalf works relating to more than one mandal. Another compromise was that the Nyaya Panchayat would not come into force for five years. Although the bill was sent for the president's assent towards the end of 1983, it received the assent only in the second week of July 1985. Meanwhile, because of the inordinate delay in Delhi, the minister for panchayati raj in Karnataka, Abdul Nazir Sab, had to announce that he would undertake a fast in front of the *Rashtrapati Bhawan* (the president of India's official residence) if the assent was not given by the president. This delay was interpreted as an instance of the central leadership's apathy towards the radical devolution of power to the people. The Karnataka Act 20 of 1985 was published in a gazette extraordinary on 2 August 1985 and was brought into force with effect from 14 August 1985.

Karnataka is the second state after West Bengal which has proclaimed its full faith in the devolution of authority on panchayati raj. The most important aspects of the act of 1985 were:

1. The district rural development authorities constituted for implementation of poverty alleviation programmes shall be abolished on the setting up of zilla parishads and their functions, assets and liabilities shall stand transferred to the zilla parishads. The functions of district planning and of the district officers of all development departments would be transferred under the control of the zilla parishads which will have as their chief executive a chief secretary, thus clearly giving the zilla parishads the slant of a district government.
2. The first point of real decentralisation below the state will be the district. This accords with the Asoka Mehta committee recommendations.
3. The zilla parishads will be based on direct elections.
4. The chairmen of the zilla parishads will be chosen from the directly elected members.
5. There will be only one tier below the district with executive functions, namely, the mandal panchayat, with the role of the middle tier of the Taluk Panchayat Samiti being mainly supervisory and for coordinating.

The act had been hailed in the press as "revolutionary in concept and wide in its sweep" (Chandrashekar 1984; *The Hindu,* 21 February 1986). The question uppermost in the minds of all was whether people in the villages of Karnataka were ready to fully utilise the radical provisions of the new act. Many had expressed apprehension as to whether the act would remain only on paper or whether it would be implemented with the people's participation. Spokesmen from Karnataka were confident that it would work well in the given context of the state and they cited several examples of people's enthusiasm and excitement over this act. Minister Abdul Nazir Sab even proclaimed that one of the reasons for the victory of his party in the 1985 elections was this act and the people's expectations from it.

Those who specialise in the area of local government finance were apprehensive whether such an ambitious system would function without adequate financial support. The argument put forward by these people was that without the basic economic reforms necessary to make the panchayati raj institutions financially viable no local self-government legislation can succeed. Karnataka is no exception to this, despite the fact that the government agreed to allocate ten rupees per annum per person residing in the mandal, calculated on the basis of the preceding census.

What was to be the role of the civil servants in the panchayat institutions? Could they not throttle the initiative? Were they not hurt because the rural folk had now become their masters under the new dispensation? The experience of the panchayati raj institutions at the national level in the post-1960 period could be an uncomfortable reminder to the Karnataka government. Moreover, unlike in many other states, the bureaucracy in Karnataka has a good record of working in the people's interests. It was reported that in that state the bureaucracy had begun to ask: What wrong have we done to be by-passed and for the powers to be given to the people's organisations? The only answer is: the bureaucracy must move with the march of time.

The issue sometimes gets clouded when spokesmen of some voluntary organisations working in rural areas point out that they prefer to deal with the district collectors and senior government officials rather than with the unsophisticated, rugged villagers, that is to say, these middle class, English-educated social workers and activists are more at home with their own class in the bureaucracy than with the villagers. This line of thinking can only give credence to officialdom at the expense of elected village bodies and also undermine the well-intentioned moves at the political level.

Other questions which came up frequently were: Into whose hands would these village bodies pass? Would they not get entrenched with the dominant castes, say, the Lingayats and Vokkaligas in Karnataka's villages? How far would the provisions of adequate representation for the Scheduled Castes and Scheduled Tribes be adhered to? Would they not be flouted with impunity? The answer to these questions was that in Karnataka the politicisation of the once oppressed castes had reached a point where it was no longer easy to dominate these village bodies in all places and at all times.

The Fallout of the 1983 Act

An interesting consequence of the Karnataka act was that it generated considerable debate in the country, not only in political circles, but in the intellectual and academic world as well. The popular response to this act in Karnataka was also taken note of by the national leadership. A renewed interest in panchayati raj could be noticed. The prime minister expressed an explicit interest in panchayati raj institutions on 14 August 1985 and wrote to all the chief ministers requesting them to hold regular elections to these bodies and give them administrative and financial support. Subsequently, India's vice-president, R. Venkataraman, while delivering the 10th Govind Ballabh Pant Memorial Lecture, pleaded for amending the constitution to make it mandatory to hold elections to the panchayats, as in the case of state legislatures and parliament (*The Hindustan Times*, 14 December 1985). He emphasized that panchayat raj institutions were the only way to ensure people's participation in the planning process. The G.V.K. Rao committee had strongly recommended that 1986 be declared the year of panchayati raj (CAARD 1985: 41). But unfortunately, these remained pious declarations for public consumption and the top-level leadership had no political will to impose panchayati raj nationwide.

In the early years of India's independence, the philosophy of governance was guided by the conviction that people are the "subjects" and not the "objects" of governance.

> Government depends on the people for authority. It is elected by the people; responsible for its actions to the people. It has to act at the behest of the people. To lead people towards the goal of the people's state, dependence should not be solely on the army of government officers. There is in that case the danger of the state owning the people and not vice versa. People should not only own and wield political power, but guide and control the economic apparatus for their well being as well. In fact, these two should go hand in hand (Government of India 1960:2).

These words were not from the pen of any revolutionary or visionary writer. In fact they came from the ministry of community development and cooperation of the government of India in the early sixties.

A quarter of a century later, sadly enough, we have moved farther away from this ideal. Rather, an ideology is now gaining ground that people are "objects" of the state and the grip of the state over the people should be tightened efficiently through intensive capitalist development with the help of high technology. In such a politically bewildering situation, the bold and principled moves made by states like Karnataka were the silver lining on an otherwise dark horizon. It was in the interest of India and its materially impoverished majority that Karnataka's experiment turn out to be an irreversible success. But the post 1991 history (up to 1994) tells another story.

7

The 1987 Panchayat Elections

The panchayati raj act (1983) of Karnataka had attracted nationwide attention because of its radical provisions relating to the devolution of power to the districts and the villages. The elections held under the new dispensation were no less important than the act itself as they threw up several significant social and political issues.

The meeting of about sixty thousand elected representatives from the panchayats and zilla parishads in Bangalore on 31 January 1987 had been a historic occasion because it had heralded the operational phase of the trail-blazing experiment. No longer was it necessary for the representatives to travel to the state capital to get things done for their districts, talukas or villages. They would now have the power and resources under their command.

The elections, held on 2 January 1987 for the zilla parishads and on 20 January 1987 for the mandal panchayats, marked the first phase to operationalise the provisions of the act. Soon after the bill had received the president's assent in 1985 the act had been enforced. It had been a stupendous task for the state machinery, to have to finalise within a short time the delimitation procedures of the constituencies for the 885 seats in the zilla parishads, the 54,688 seats in the mandal panchayats, and the lists of voters, including the eighteen-year old who got the voting rights for the first time.

I had been keen to observe how the village folk had responded to the new measure. A visit to the interiors of Mysore, Hunsur and H.D.Kote talukas during the second (mandal) polls turned out to be an enriching experience. Enthusiastic voters had lined up at the booths early in the morning, women out-numbering men in most places. The fact that just a few days earlier they had been required to stand in the queue for another poll had not dampened their enthusiasm. The turn out of voters for the mandal polls had been higher in spite of the harvest work. (The average turn out for the earlier zilla parishads polls had been only 60 percent, but for the mandals it was 75 percent.)

One of the complaints aired about the panchayat poll from many quarters had been that the elections, having been held on party lines, had introduced serious rifts in the otherwise harmonious village life of Karnataka, and had affected individual families. For instance, if the father in a certain family was a Congress(I) supporter, the sons were discovered to be with the Janata; if a daughter-in-law was for the Janata, the mother-in-law was for the Congress(I). In Devanahalli the wives of two brothers had stood for the elections. All this had created tension in the villages, even resulting in some clashes, so much so that these elections came to be characterised as *kolaku mandala* (dirty mandal) elections. Elderly people said that they had never witnessed such restlessness in villages in the wake of elections. But those who make a fetish of village harmony during elections forget the antagonism and conflicts between caste groups, and the haves and have-nots at a subterranean level. As Abdul Nazir Sab put it, anyway, in the villages there is "Ramanna and Bhimanna politics." It is a reality. Isn't it healthier that people align on democratic, party lines rather than on the basis of caste, religion, and so on?

Interestingly, the perceptions about village peace varied from person to person. In a village in Shimoga, a 75-year old farmer, Gidappa, said that he hated the Janata party as its tendency to help only the *Harijans* (literally, the children of god, a term used by Gandhi for the lower castes) had disturbed the peace in the village. In at least ten villages of Bengapalli, near Bangalore, the Scheduled Caste candidates had filed their nominations from unreserved constituencies. Many elders considered this to be very uncommon and an act of defiance. In some places the upper castes had threatened the SC candidates, demanding that they should confine themselves to the reserved constituencies but finally the upper castes had to take back their own words. All this reinforces the conflict model of social transformation.

Drawbacks of Partyless Democracy

There is no doubt that the discussion and debates in village tea shops and market-places had been elevated to the level of political ideologies, assessment of the balance sheets of the political parties and of the track record of political leaders–all this because the elections had been held on party lines. The elections proved to be a churning process of ideas and actions, creating a high level of political consciousness. If political parties are indispensable for parliamentary democracy, is it not important that they must take root in the villages, through elections based on party lines?

The danger of a partyless democracy in the villages is that the entire village may come to depend on the one individual who dominates by virtue of his caste, family, money-power or musclemen. The Kagodu village in Shimoga, for instance, had never seen elections to the panchayat for the last twenty years. The village was dominated by a political leader and he used to be elected "unanimously."

In the 1987 elections also this "unanimity" manifested itself in a big way. About 20 percent of the Mandal Panchayat seats were found to be filled by "consensus" candidates. This unusually large number of unopposed candidates was puzzling to many. Some explained it away by saying that it reflected the collective wisdom and common will that prevails in the villages. Going a step further, some also said that this indicated the villagers unanimity over persons with a "clean" record. Even if there is an element of truth in all this, the dominant reality–the coercive power of traditional caste alignments, of bullies and money-power–cannot be sidetracked. There is a stronger probability that those who were elected under the SC, ST and womens' quota may turn out to be the henchmen or puppets of the strong and the powerful individuals. Anyway, this does not diminish the significance of the election's potential to unleash forces which will eventually recognise the dignity, rights and abilities of every person. It is a vision for the future and viewed from that perspective, the Karnataka elections were a watershed.

There was no doubt that these local-level elections promoted the leaders from the dominant castes. Lingayat candidates got elected where this caste was powerful. Vokkaligas cashed in on the areas where they dominate. Since in many villages no single community could ensure a victory for its candidate, it sought alliances with others. This paved the way for polarisation on party lines. It was observed in Karnataka that if the Zilla Parishad elections showed a new trend, with the vote cutting across caste barriers, the Mandal Panchayat elections marked the new trend of votes cutting through family ties.

Popular Response

The elections have also manifested some interesting social and anthropological aspects of village life. Some candidates had sold their milch animals–the main source of their income–to raise money for election expenses. In most of the booths that I visited, ballot boxes had been garlanded, *kum kum* (the vermilion powder applied on the forehead) applied to them and fruits, including bananas and coconuts, kept by the side. The candidate himself, or an elder representing his party, would come early in the morning to be ahead of others so that he could perform the *puja* (worship) first. In some places, persons representing rival parties competed for the first place to perform the puja. At a booth in the Mysore Taluk the presiding officer told me how he managed to avert an ugly scene by permitting both the parties to perform puja at the same time. Since a Mandal Panchayat member represents just four to six hundred members he knows everybody in his constituency by face and in turn his constituency is also familiar with him. Therefore, integrity and honesty have a great role to play. In many booths the candidates themselves were the polling agents. There were also the usual cases of some villagers boycotting the elections to protest against neglect in the past by the elected representatives of parties.

Ignorance among many of the implications of the new panchayati raj was evident. Several candidates confessed that they were not familiar with the new law or its interpretations, nor had they a grasp of the powers vested in these institutions. Several women candidates, though illiterate, had contested because someone influential had asked them to do so. Even the acknowledged leaders were not sure of the new law. A former chief minister, who later became a minister at the centre, used to proclaim in public (obviously in an attempt to misinform) that under the new dispensation fresh taxes would be levied by the zilla parishads! The state government should get the credit for spending considerable time and money to help the elected representatives understand the implications of the new legislation.

The elections revealed the people's preference for a two-party system. The choice was either for the Janata party or the Congress(I), and that too on a fairly even scale. When, for the Zilla Parishad elections, the Janata got 449 seats, the Congress(I) ran close to secure 395 seats. In the second elections, the Janata party party won 27,333 seats and the Congress(i) 20,697 seats. It seems the people of Karnataka have realised that one-party rule can be a curse for democracy. A strong opposition is the cornerstone of a vibrant democratic polity. Ramakrishna Hegde, Karnataka's chief minister at the time, had been advocating this at the national level then and the panchayat elections of 1987 in Karnataka seemed to show that the people of the state had followed the wishes of their chief minister. The BJP, CPI, and the CPI(M) failed to make any impact in these elections. The BJP secured only 1.1 percent of the votes in the mandals. However, in these lower level tiers, a substantially large number of independents were elected, securing about 10 percent votes. For example, in Tumkur all the 214 candidates elected unopposed were independents. This phenomenon is evidence of the non-party political process that still grips village life.

Another vocal issue was the oft-repeated accusation that the Janata government had been giving too much power to the village bodies. Not only the bureaucracy but the M.L.As had also felt agitated about the erosion of their power and prestige. But the relentless Ramakrishna Hegde had been convinced that the powers given to the grassroots level bodies would only help to evolve a better system. At a meeting of Karnataka government officials, prior to the elections, some of these officials had been visibly upset over the suggestion to award the designation "chief secretary" to the senior-most official in the rural, Zilla Parishad services. Even V.K.R.V. Rao (the eminent educationist) shared their fears and suggested that such an official could be called the chief executive. Intervening in the discussion, Hegde had retorted that he, to the contrary, would have had no objection to even calling the adhyaksh of the Zilla Parishad the chief minister of the district!

8

Is Panchayati Raj Withering Away in Karnataka?

Perhaps no other local self-government experiment attracted the nationwide media and the attention of international scholars as that of Karnataka where the first Zilla Parishad and Mandal Panchayat bodies were elected in January 1987. West Bengal was the other state which caught the attention of national and international observers but in the latter case it was more for the continued existence of panchayati raj in the last fourteen years as the unit of local self-government rather than for its radical nature. The Karnataka panchayati raj act of 1983 was a definite improvement on the West Bengal model. That the government at the centre at that time found the act uncomfortable was evident from the fact that it took more than one year for the president to give his assent.

Reverses in the 1983 Act

The acclaim which the Karnataka model received internationally was reflected in an important international symposium held in 1992 in the capital on "Perspectives on India's Development in the 1990s." The president of the Ford Foundation, Franklin A. Thomas, had spoken in his address about Karnataka's decentralisation as a very promising experiment. He had said:

> A first step towards building a more supportive institutional structure for development in India must involve government decentralisation. A very promising experiment with state-local decentralisation has been taking place in Karnataka. Under the Karnataka set up, local elected councils have been given real decision-making power over local development plans and programs. Initial evaluations of this system show that the

> elected councils have been more responsible to their constituents' needs than the appointed administrators were under the previous system. The district and sub-district councils have also played an important role in nurturing new political participants, especially women and members of disadvantaged castes...it seems clear that the concept of democratic decentralisation has been proven effective in Karnataka and deserves to be considered more widely.

Even as Franklin Thomas was telling his august audience how the elected councils had been more responsible to their constituents' needs than the appointed administrators, the government in Karnataka (and the chief minister, Bangarappa), had finalised and begun implementing administrator's raj in place of panchayati raj. Today the story of Karnataka's panchayati raj is Bangarappa's success and the people's failure. As soon as the five-year term of the elected representatives expired, the government prepared the way for the administrators to step in and take over the local bodies. Thus the government "killed" the system.

But the emasculation of panchayati raj in Karnataka has brought to the fore certain issues which are pertinent to the growth and survival of grassroots-level democracy and of the Indian polity.

First, the question of political will, on which volumes have been written. From the day the Congress(I) came to power in Karnataka in November 1989, it was uncomfortable with the zilla parishads and mandal panchayats which were seen as the legacy of Janata rule in the state. The Congress(I) rulers in the state began to look at panchayati raj through myopic eyes, although it had been functioning according to an act passed by a legislature which had seen their own party fare well in the elections. (The 38.03 percent seats of the mandals and the 44.53 percent seats of the zilla parishads had been won by the Congress party.)

The initial salvo had been fired in November 1990 when the Congress(I) had introduced a bill in the assembly to amend the Karnataka panchayati raj act of 1983. The changes to be introduced had been finalised by the Congress(I) Legislature party executive earlier, in September itself. This move was meant to alter the basic features of the four-year old panchayati raj system, vesting more powers in bureaucrats by sidelining the elected representatives. Following a hue and cry from all concerned, including a section of the Congress(I) itself, and through the intervention of Rajiv Gandhi (in his capacity as president of the Congress party) in response to a memorandum submitted to him in person by the Zilla Parishad chairpersons, the move, initiated at the instance of Bangarappa, was temporarily stalled. After the 1991 parliamentary elections the latter was at his games again. Instead of making preparations for holding the elections so that the newly elected representatives could take over in January 1992, his government was drafting an ordinance to subvert the panchayati raj system. The ordinance became the act of 1993 (receiving the governor's assent on 21 March). The passage of the bill itself had made history. It had been taken up in the Legislative Assembly on 21 March and passed in just thirty minutes, at a time when the entire opposition had boycotted the session because of the leakage of the budget proposals. The bill had been defeated in the Legislative Council and again returned to the assembly. But when it went back to the council it was defeated for the second time!

All this undue haste was just to place the panchayats in the hands of bureaucrats. The relevant amendment axing the role of people's representatives had stated that if the term of the outgoing members of the Zilla Parishad has expired and the new Zilla Parishad has not been constituted in accordance with the provisions of this act, the government shall, by notification, appoint an administrator for such period as may be specified in the notification and may, by like notification, curtail or *extend* the period of such appointment (emphasis added). Further, it had also stated that on the appointment of an administrator under sub-section (1), all the powers and duties of the adhyaksha or upadhyaksha, and the Zilla Parishad and committees thereof shall be exercised and performed by such administrators.

Premature Decisions

It is nobody's case that the Karnataka panchayati raj act of 1983 is sacrosanct. The evaluation committee (K.S. Krishnaswamy committee) appointed by the Karnataka government, in its report submitted in 1989, was of the view that panchayati raj, as visualised by the 1983 act, should be tried for some time before any major change in it is attempted, since both the state government and the local governments had not had enough time to get attuned to the new situation. An independent study made in 1990 by the Institute of Social Sciences, New Delhi, had come to the conclusion that at that point of time, it seemed a little premature to suggest major changes in the panchayati raj act, considering the fact that the new panchayati raj had been functioning only since April 1987. It would have been more appropriate to give it a chance, and let it function for at least one full term (i.e., till 1992) before amending the act. Bangarappa and his ministerial colleagues, of course, decided to move in the opposite direction.

It is common knowledge that after Nehru no one in the Congress party really believed in panchayati raj; to the contrary all possible efforts were made to concentrate power in Delhi. When the seventy-second constitution amendment bill (which had several positive suggestions for strengthening local self-government) was introduced in parliament by the government headed by Narasimha Rao in 1991, it was hailed as a bold step in the correct direction. Yet, although one year passed following its introduction, it was not taken up for debate, as it remained with the select committee. One would, at the time, have liked to give the benefit of doubt to Prime Minister Narasimha Rao. But then, one fails to understand why the same prime minister did not raise any objection to his Karnataka chief minister's misadventure with local self-government? Why these double standards?

The second area of discussion relevant for our polity refers to the criticism of skeptics who insist on knowing what the Karnataka panchayati raj institutions had really achieved? Were they not also centres of corruption? The attempts to run down the achievements of Karnataka in this field are reminiscent of the immediate post-Nehruvian days. Objective studies of the decline of panchayati raj in the mid-sixties, as mentioned earlier, had shown that there were deliberate plans made by the bureaucracy, local vested interests and their elected representatives in the assemblies and in parliament, to cripple and eventually discard panchayati raj, the ascendancy of which was feared by them. History is repeating itself in Karnataka.

The Achievements

As has been mentioned, there are no two opinions that Karnataka's panchayati raj had several firsts to its credit and its achievements were not mean by any measure. At a meeting of Zilla Parishad and Mandal Panchayat pradhans, convened by the Bangalore rural Zilla Parishad in the first week of January 1992 to evaluate the performance of the pradhans (this writer was also present at the two day function), and to bid adieu to a system which had been subverted by Bangarappa, it was a delight to witness rustic leaders (men and women) from all over the state coming up and addressing the gathering. Their leadership, boldness and sense of achievement were specially noteworthy. There was general agreement that in the last five years resource mobilisation had been excellent, and sources untapped earlier had been tapped. Works, which had not been taken up for thirty to forty years, had been implemented during the term in office of these leaders. A woman member from Neelamangala had recounted that till the new panchayati raj came into existence she was the only woman in that area who used to come out in public and the people used to laugh at her for doing so. But after five years of panchayati raj the situation had changed dramatically; many women now participated in the affairs of the village, as now a congenial ethos existed for it.

One pradhan, who came from a distant mandal, challenged the government to bring out a white paper on the working of zilla parishads and mandals. He said that what the government had taken forty years to do from Bangalore, these local bodies had done in five years and their work had been superior. A Congress(I) Zilla Parishad member in the Bangalore rural Zilla Parishad, who was also the leader of the opposition there, asserted that he had as much interest in retaining the system as the others. Mani Shanker Aiyar, the Congress(I) M.P. who spoke in the closing session, had pleaded with the state chief minister not to tamper with the system, considering its achievements and its potential for the future of our democracy.

The question of corruption at the Zilla Parishad and Mandal Panchayat levels has been mentioned again and again. For instance, "misappropriation and misapplication of funds" was given as one of the four major irregularities attributed to zilla parishads and the mandals and to set it right the Congress(I) government had found it necessary to bring amendments to the 1983 act. There is no doubt that there is corruption below the state level. Earlier corruption occurred without the people knowing about it. Today also this can be found in the panchayat institutions, but now people are in the know of things. Since the districts and mandals are smaller units, but with a large number of people's representatives functioning as watchdogs, nothing can be hidden from their watchful eyes. If a case is built up by using charges of corruption in order to scrap the system or diminish the importance of people's representatives, this is tantamount to throwing the baby away with the bath water. After all, in a democracy, isn't it the people who should punish their corrupt and wicked representatives as and when the next elections take place? Instead, these very elections are postponed indefinitely. What kind of logic is this?

In West Bengal too there have been, and continue to be charges of corruption against the local bodies, but the state also serves as an example of how regularity of elections provide in-built mechanisms to constrain the scope of wrongdoing. In an illuminating study which used the example of West Bengal, John Echeverri-Gent (of Virginia University) had observed that while the political process provides avenues for corruption, it also creates mechanisms to constrain the scope of corruption. Voters use electoral sanctions to a remarkable extent against panchayat members with a reputation for corruption. In Moyna block, according to Gent, the CPI(M) had dominated local politics ever since 1977. It won the panchayat elections in 1978. It defeated the Congress(I) in the 1982 legislative assembly elections for the Moyna constituency by ten thousand votes. The party stemmed the tide in favor of Rajiv Gandhi by winning two thousand votes more than the Congress(I) in the Lok Sabha elections in 1984. Yet it lost the panchayat elections in 1983 when the Congress(I) won control over seven of the block's eleven gram panchayats. What is the reason for this anomaly, Gent asks? The most persuasive explanation for Gent was that since three CPI(M) pradhans had become mired in charges of corruption, this had created a popular backlash against the party at the local level, causing its defeat.

A similar situation, according to Gent, had cropped up in Binpur I. The CPI(M) had won control over the ten gram panchayats in the block in the 1978 elections. Corruption had become an issue in the 1983 campaign. Binpur I is divided by the Kasai river. Four gram panchayats are located east of the Kasai, and six to the west. The CPI(M) was criticised for channelling funds and benefits to the four eastern gram panchayats and neglecting the six in the west. This tendency was encouraged by the fact that there were two CPI(M) local committees for the block–one for the east and one for the west. The sabhapati of the block's Panchayat Samiti was also the secretary of the party's local committee for the east. By channeling disproportionate benefits to his home base, he alienated the six *anchals* (a conglomeration of villages) to the west. In the 1983 elections, the opposition defeated the CPI(M) in all the six western gram panchayats.

A natural query that arises from this account of West Bengal is, why did the Karnataka government not take the corrupt adhyakshas, pradhans or the members to the people's court? It is not difficult to see that the real force behind the drive to wipe out panchayati raj were the M.L.As. It is they who discredited the experiment by saying that it had nothing but vices and that zilla parishads and mandals were the embodiment of failures and failures alone. This was perhaps because the M.L.As' wings were being clipped by decentralisation below the state level. Even the Janata Dal M.L.As were not fully convinced of the rationale for the erosion of their power and status. How can lesser mortals–the small village leaders–usurp their (the M.L.As) power "to hold all that they surveyed," the latter would ask? Even the M.Ps seemed to share the concern of their brethren at the state-level. So, behind a Narasimha Rao or a Bangarappa one could discern the unseen hands of the M.L.As and M.Ps who were disgruntled at the thought of others sharing their power. The Karnataka episode is a clear example of this unsavoury development, which seems to have become a national phenomenon.

Implications for the Future

The suppression of panchayati raj in Karnataka, and related issues, has brought another crucial aspect to the forefront which has a bearing on the development of our future political process. This relates to the exemplary role of the judiciary in upholding the principles of grassroots-level democracy. When legislatures, possessing the brute majority of the ruling parties, become blind to social realities, they tend to ignore constitutional niceties and sometimes make laws which violate the civilised existence of societies. The judiciary in India has been setting things right whenever legislatures have been acting arbitrarily.

The judgement delivered by the Karnataka High Court Division Bench, on a writ petition presented by fifteen citizens who were aggrieved by the indefinite postponement of elections to the zilla parishads in the state, is a classic one but has not received the coverage it deserves. The High Court's verdict should open the eyes of all practising politicians. The court said that the enormous power and functions conferred on the Zilla Parishad, read in conjunction with its democratic structure, point to the devolution of such power on the zilla parishads for the purpose of securing the real panchayati raj system of Mahatma Gandhi's dream. The judges even reprimanded the petitioners for rushing to the court too late and concluded that at a time when there was no visible action on the part of the government to hold elections, the elected representatives had kept quiet in the hope of getting their term extended for another six months because there was no provision in the act to appoint an administrator. The case, observed the judges, was an example of what could happen if the citizens were not vigilant and did not resort to constitutional remedies in good time. The citizens would have to suffer heavy losses, the judges continued, to wit, the loss of democratic, local self-government, at least for the successive annual term. In their opinion, in the case under review, an invaluable right had been lost for want of vigilance.

Another outstanding judgement of the division branch of the Allahabad High Court in the case of Anugrah Narain Singh v. State of Uttar Pradesh (1962) was extensively quoted by the two judges, Rama Jois and N.J. Hanumanthappa. The main grievance of the petitioners before the Allahabad High Court was that for long periods of time no elections were held to the municipalities in the state while the government had been taking the stand that it had the freedom of choice in holding or not holding elections to local bodies. In its enlightened judgement the court ruled that local self-government was a basic feature of the constitution of India and that *the citizens are entitled as of right to have elected representatives only to administer them* (that is, these local bodies) and any existence of, or exercise of, arbitrary power by the government was unconstitutional. Local self-government was the arch upon which parliamentary democracy in this nation rested and upon it the dome with state legislatures and the federal parliament. The structure would collapse without the arches. Even the legislature ought not to and cannot legislate to kill local self-government; that it may is another matter, warned one of the best judgements on the subject. Sadly enough, some states, including Uttar Pradesh, considered it expedient to ignore these profound words both in letter and in spirit.

After the Allahabad judgement, it is the Karnataka High Court's erudite judgement which makes essential reading for all those even remotely concerned with our democracy. In the eyes of the judges the postponement of the general elections to all zilla parishads was not a simple matter as it rendered a severe blow to the democratic system. The inaction–not holding the election–and the action of placing local self-government in the hands of civil servants would have robbed the local body of its democratic character. It would have become merely a local government and would have ceased to be local *self-government.* Therefore the obligation imposed by the act on the government was "to hold elections in time to ensure that at all times the zilla parishads are administered by the people's representatives." The High Court ordered that elections to zilla parishads be held before 31 December 1992. The state government did not go on appeal to the Supreme Court for quite some time.

The state government's main objection to holding elections to the panchayat bodies in 1991 had been that since the 72nd Constitution Amendment Bill had been introduced in parliament in 1991, after it became a law the state act would, in any case, have had to be amended in accordance with the provisions of the central act. The simple question is: If by some unforeseen developments the constitutional amendment were to take several years to become law (as it did in the case of the sixty-fourth amendment), then ought all those states with functioning panchayati raj have come to a halt because of the likelihood of a new act coming up? In such a situation, none of the local self-governments would have been able to hold elections till such time that the president of India gave his assent to the said act. The High Court was amused by this argument put forward by the Karnataka state government because the very purpose of the central government's move for a constitutional amendment had been to ensure regular elections to local bodies. Earlier that year the neighbouring state of Maharashtra had held the elections to the panchayats. Orissa had successfully held the municipal elections and the panchayat elections were in the process of being completed at the time. Could the Maharashtra and Orissa governments be regarded as foolish and the Karnataka government wiser?

The High Court had also intervened decisively in the case of mandal panchayats. A writ petition had been pending before the court but it proceeded to grant an interim stay to more than one thousand mandals against the operation of the government notification appointing administrators. (According to the Karnataka act of 1983, the pradhans continue in office till new ones are elected and assume office. The new act of 1992 has removed this clause, but that is another matter.) The administrators who had taken over the mandals had to vacate for the pradhans and there were instances of administrators refusing to quit and of the pradhans having to initiate contempt of court proceedings before they could be re-instated.

In the well attended final meeting of panchayati raj representatives in Bangalore on 10 January 1992, on the eve of their laying down office, C. Narayanaswamy, chairman of the Bangalore rural Zilla Parishad, had noted in his farewell speech that the zilla parishads had tried a lot, achieved a lot. They had created awareness in the villages. The state government may have had might, but people all over needed power and craved for decentralisation. Governments must see the writing on the wall, he had warned. This outpouring was spontaneous; there was a touch of sincerity in it. But if governments close their eyes to the writing on the wall and the opposition parties are caught up in personality clashes and inertia, what will happen to the people's craving for democracy?

Every right-thinking person knows that for the sake of democracy in the country, Karnataka's panchayati raj experiment should not be allowed to fail. The situation in Karnataka is ripe today for a movement to flower on this very issue of the deliberate destruction of local self-government by the state government. But the people are not organised around this question. The main opposition in the state at the time (in 1992), the Janata Dal, was in too poor a health to lead a movement. Therefore the people are back to square one.

9

Karnataka Puts the Clock Back

Whether the elephants make love or they fight, it is the grass that suffers. It now seems clear that local self-government, and consequently the common people in the villages of Karnataka, have been made the victims of petty politics, prejudices and the love-hate relationship of politicians of various hues in the state.

The 1993 Act

The Karnataka Panchayati Raj Act, 1993, is a severe blow to the ideal of transforming panchayats into units of self-government and revitalising them, as visualised in the seventy-third constitution amendment act of 1992. This had been the essence of this constitutional amendment. Those who wanted to throw out the much acclaimed Karnataka model of decentralisation (enshrined in its 1983 act), have done it lock, stock and barrel, and with a vengeance, notwithstanding the promises given on the floor of the Legislative Council by the government that suitable amends will be made in due course. What the state has got ultimately in the name of panchayati raj is form without content.

What are the obnoxious features of this bill which subverts the essence of the local government system? The Directive Principles of State Policy in the constitution (Article 40) and the seventy-third amendment are categorical that panchayati raj institutions are "units/institutions of self-government." So governance through local bodies below the state level is the crux of the problem. But the recent Karnataka act, in its preamble, has ignored this vital principle and reduced the panchayat bodies to the level of rural development bodies. It says that the panchayats are being established "for greater participation of the people and *more effective implementation of rural development programmes*" (emphasis added).

Almost all the committees which looked into the question of the relationship between elected local bodies and the officials have highlighted the principle that the interface between elected functionaries of panchayat institutions and officials should accord primacy to accountability by the officials to the people's representatives. Since independence, the non-functioning and moribund democratic institutions below the state level have created a perverted attitude among the officials as well as state level political leaders to show a preference for officers raj but under the garb of helping the grassroots-level democratic institutions.

The most celebrated feature of the 1983 Karnataka act was that it was the first radical attempt in the country to pass on governance to people's representatives below the state level. Thus, due to this act, the adhyaksha of a Zilla Parishad came to enjoy the status of a minister of state, and the upadhyaksha that of a deputy minister, a fact which symbolised the attempts to recognise the sovereignty of the people. The administrators were placed under the adhyakshas who were to exercise supervision and control *over* the officers and employees.

Breach of a Basic Principle

The 1993 act is a serious breach of this basic principle of democracy. While the act gives the adhyaksha of a Grama Panchayat the same powers as in the 1983 act, similar powers are *not* given to the adhyaksha of a Taluk Panchayat or a Zilla Parishad. The present government has deliberately reduced the position of the Zilla Parishad (now Zilla Panchayat) adhyaksha from that of an "executive head" to one "exercising supervision and control over the executive officer for securing implementation of resolutions or decisions." Thus the chairpersons have been made weak and titular. The situation is rendered all the more absurd and vulnerable in cases where the adhyaksha belongs to either the SCs, STs or is a woman. Obviously, the party in power in the state does not trust the chiefs of the local bodies in the use of their powers.

At the same time, the Karnataka act has a chapter entitled "Inspection, Supervision," which details the powers of officialdom. This chapter has detailed those powers of officers which will have a devastating effect on the functioning of the local bodies. Take, for instance, the provision which empowers officials (through an order of the government, of course) to enquire into the affairs of grama panchayats, taluk panchayats and zilla panchayats. The officers have the powers of the civil courts under the code of civil procedure and their verdict has to be executed as if it were a decree of the civil court! More damaging is the power given to the chief executive officer (CEO) under Article 237 of the act. If, in the opinion of the CEO, the execution of any order of a Grama Panchayat is "unjust" and so on, then "he may order or suspend the execution or prohibit the doing thereof." This power in the case of taluk panchayats vests in the commissioners, and for zilla panchayats in the government. Thus the act makes the officer the arbiter and his judgement is made more important than the collective wisdom of the elected representatives of the panchayat.

While there are clear provisions in the 1983 act to give powers to the zilla parishads and their functionaries regarding postings, recruitment, transfer of and administrative control over the officials, the related provision regarding administrative powers and authority in the new act have been taken away from the purview of the taluk panchayats and zilla panchayats. It may be noted that Section 155(3) of the 1993 act states:

> Notwithstanding anything contained in this act or any other law for the time being in force, Government or any officer or other authority authorised by it in this behalf shall have power to effect transfer of the officers and officials so posted either within the Taluk or from one Taluk to another Taluk.

In other words, even the transfer of a peon in the panchayat or a Zilla Panchayat will now rest with the officer. Wherever the term government is used, it is, for all practical purposes, a euphemism for officers at the district and lower levels. It also conveniently legitimises ministerial-level interference and hence opens the Pandora's box. Karnataka has now shown the way as to how there should not be any administrative power or control for elected functionaries of the panchayat. In sum, the panchayats have been in no uncertain terms made subservient to the officials and an appendage of the state government. We may recall here the Sadiq Ali committee's observation on this question thirty years ago while reviewing the functioning of panchayati raj in Rajasthan at the behest of the state government. In 1964 the committee had observed:

> The elected representatives should recognise that it is the right of the officers to offer their advice on policy and that they are expected to do so. At the same time, it should be recognised by the officers that it is well within the right of the elected representatives to reject their (the officers) advice (see Jain et al. 1985:40).

A more serious lapse refers to the amendment section of the act. The constitutional amendment empowers the state legislature to give powers and functions to the panchayats. But Section 312 of the Karnataka act vests the power to "omit, amend or add any activity, programme or scheme covered by or mentioned in Schedule I, II or III," in the government. It can be done by notification in the gazette and later on all that the government has to do is just to place it before the legislature. This provision makes the powers and functions of the panchayats dependent on the sweet will of the governments of the time, sabotaging the very concept of self-government.

Till today, for several states the Karnataka panchayati raj act of 1983 had been a reference point. But the new act of 1993 adopted by the assembly has destroyed that honour. The National Institute of Rural Development (NIRD) in Hyderabad has just brought out a model bill for states which is inspired on the seventy-third constitutional amendment act. This is a far more progressive and pro-people measure. The intelligentsia and opinion-makers may do well to warn other states against imitating Karnataka's "pro-officers raj" act.

Part Three

The Experience of Orissa, West Bengal and China

10

Orissa Leads the Way

Alexis de Tocqueville once characterised elections as "institutionalised revolutions." When a determined Biju Patnaik, during his second term as the chief minister of Orissa (since 1990), wanted to awaken the state from its backwardness and apathy he realised that without grassroots-level democracy nothing could be achieved. Therefore, he went ahead with elections to the municipalities, grama panchayats and panchayat samitis–much against the wishes of the M.L.As, including those from his own party. This happened in early 1992 but it assumed the proportions of an institutionalised revolution in the state, as was evident on 5 March 1993, the birthday of Biju *Da,* when Bhubaneswar was spruced up to celebrate the "Panchayatiraj Divas"(panchayatiraj day). The assembly of about sixteen thousand elected representatives of panchayats–all the chairpersons, vice-chairpersons and members of panchayat samitis, all the sarpanches and *naib* (deputy) sarpanches of gram panchayats, along with the M.L.As and M.Ps from the state, the government officials and the invitees–who deliberated at the Kalinga Stadium for two days on the new panchayat, resuscitated after a lapse of twelve years, was a historic one.

Prior to this, such assemblies had taken place in the country only twice. The first had taken place in Orissa itself when Biju Patnaik had become the chief minister for the first time (1961-63). At the time he was of the view that every sarpanch must function like the chief minister of his panchayat so that people would hold him or her in respect. He brought together eight thousand sarpanches in Bhubaneswar for a conference and told them to function as representatives of the state. The second such meeting took place in 1987 in Karnataka State. Chief Minister Ramakrishna Hegde brought together in Bangalore the fifty-six thousand Zilla Parishad and Mandal Panchayat members who had been elected according to the new panchayat act of 1983 introduced by the Janata government. Incidentally, that great convention of people's representatives was inaugurated by the present prime minister, P. V. Narasimha Rao (who was a union cabinet minister then), brushing aside the protests of local Congress leaders who insisted on warning him that he was falling into the trap of Ramakrishna Hegde!

Empowering Women

What made the recent Bhubaneswar meeting significant was that almost half the participants were women. Orissa has been the first state to implement 33 percent reservation of seats for women in municipalities and panchayats, at a time when the centre was still only deliberating on this issue. Thus, Orissa has now about 480 women representatives in the ninety-four municipalities. They number more than twenty-five thousand in the 5,263 gram panchayats and 314 panchayat samitis. Most of the seats reserved for women were contested by several candidates. This achievement becomes all the more spectacular when seen against the background of women's literacy in the state, which is 29.1 percent only.

The Orissa gram panchayat act enables women to hold offices at all tiers of the panchayati raj institutions. Further, it has a unique provision by which if the Gram Panchayat sarpanch, elected or nominated, is not a woman, the office of the naib-sarpanch will go to a woman. A similar provision exists for the chairperson of the Panchayat Samiti. This step is a radical one, considering the fact that neither the Constitution (Seventy-third Amendment) Act of 22 December 1992, nor any other state has a provision as progressive as that of Orissa (the constitutional act has gone only so far as to state that not less than one-third of the total number of offices of chairpersons in the panchayats at each level shall be reserved for women).

The upsurge of women's power was in evidence at the Bhubaneswar meet. They boldly came forward and gave vent to their feelings and frustrations. They blamed the government for not giving them sufficient power and resources. "We are elected. That is good news. We are not able to implement anything, we have no power, no resources. That is bad news," proclaimed the women representatives in unison while addressing the huge gathering. "The bureaucracy is not responsive," was the refrain. "We women are behind you. But the bureaucracy will kill your dreams," they said. "The block development officers are not listening to the women representatives," claimed another.

The chief minister patiently listened to these voices of the people for two days; he was certainly at the receiving end. One young woman addressed him as "my son Biju" because he had characterised women in his talk as mothers (*mathru jati*).

I asked him what in his opinion was the major reason for panchayats not taking off. He said, "If the panchayat system fails, it will be because of corrupt administration. Forty-five years of independence have only strengthened a corrupt administrative system. These women who were speaking were pouring out in agony and anger against the corrupt, unresponsive administrators." In his opinion the M.L.As have come to realise, although reluctantly, that power-sharing below the state level has become a reality and they are slowly reconciling themselves to it. But the corrupt officials are the problem, according to Orissa's patriarch.

The Zilla Parishads

Orissa has had an active Zilla Parishad system since 1961. But it was abolished in 1967, when Biju's grip over the state and politics declined towards the end of the sixties, and in its place district planning boards were created by the Congress government that followed. For about twenty-five years the state had no power-sharing mechanism below the state level and it is now being recognised that this vacuum, more than any other factor, contributed to Orissa's social and economic backwardness. In 1991, the present government enacted the Orissa Zilla Parishad Act, 1991, incorporating several progressive features of self-government. The 1991 act has characteristics similar to the much acclaimed Kerala District Council Act so that the parishad members include the chairpersons of each of the urban local bodies constituted in the district, besides official and non-official members of all important elected bodies from the Panchayat Samiti upwards. Only directly elected members–two members from every block–have the power to vote. The act did not envisage giving voting rights even to M.Ps and M.L.As, but now, under the new constitutional amendment, Orissa may have to fall in line and give them voting rights, which will inflict a blow to the concept of "units of local self-government."

The Orissa government has an open mind regarding its own legislation and it goes to the credit of the present leadership that it has invited suggestions to improve the quality of these local bodies. The veteran advocate of panchayati raj, L.C. Jain, and the author had a meeting with the chief minister, his minister for panchayati raj, Damodar Raut, and senior state officials in which some suggestions were made to make the district bodies genuinely self-governing institutions. Some of these suggestions need to be mentioned here in the context of the present countrywide discussions on the subject. Regarding planning it was recommended that the planning department should work out the methodology for assimilating Zilla Parishad plans into the state plans. Second, the budgetary procedures should ensure that the allocations for zilla parishads are directly from the budget. The present practice of "district sector" budget will need to be replaced by direct lump sum allocations to zilla parishads without dividing them up into sector allocations–so that planning from below can begin to work effectively.

We felt that making the district collector the chief executive officer under the present act was not conducive to the healthy functioning of zilla parishads. In our opinion the experience of the last forty years has shown that the requirements of both development, and law and order functions at the district level, have grown enormously and will continue to grow further. At the same time the arrangement of putting these two functions in one hand–the collector's–have not yielded the expected results.

In our view, law and order (along with revenue collection and related matters) should be separated from the ever-increasing and specialised area of development and each should be placed under a separate functionary with the collector responsible for the former, and the Zilla Parishad, with a full time chief executive officer, for the latter.

Further, when zilla parishads are conceived as "units of self-government" that are expected to carry out developmental activities with political power, the chief executive officer should be a senior civil servant (senior to the collector) of the state who can work with the chairman, elected representatives and other members at the district and state levels. We must also reckon with the fact that people's expectations are bound to rise. The system of separation of the functions of the district collector and the chief executive officer of the Zilla Parishad, therefore, cannot be delayed for too long in our country.

Although the chief minister was fairly convinced that given our colonial heritage, the district collector was seen as the chief executive *par excellence* of a district by the people, it was heartening to note that the Orissa government has an open mind with regard to having a senior civil servant as the chief executive officer, as per our suggestion.

We also proposed that awards be constituted to encourage healthy competition among the zilla parishads. Of course, Biju Patnaik, in his capacity as the chief minister of Orissa in the early sixties, had made similar suggestions. But it is significant that on the "Panchayatiraj Divas" he announced that the Grama Panchayat which was rated first in each district with respect to development activities would be awarded one lakh (that is, one hundred thousand) rupees and the three best panchayat samitis selected from the three revenue divisions would get one crore (ten million) rupees to be used for further development activities.

Orissa lost some precious time in not holding the Zilla Parishad elections immediately after the Municipal, Grama Panchayat and Panchayat Samiti elections. A couple of months were lost due to the games played on the political chessboard by the ruling party, the cabinet, and so on. A genuine reason for the delay was the reorganisation of districts, an issue which had been hanging fire for some time. The thirteen districts have become seventeen now and from 1 April 1993, twenty-eight districts will start functioning. Still, the average population per district will be a formidable ten lakhs! This reorganisation was a tough task and a *sine qua non* for the zilla parishads to take root in a manageable way.

At the moment, the danger is that the political will to strengthen panchayati raj bodies and make them vibrant institutions of local self-government depends on a single person's convictions, a person who turned seventy-eight recently. The sooner his ideas become part of the system and get institutionalised the better for the future of the state. The "Panchayatiraj Divas" celebrations demonstrated that Biju Patnaik is consciously building women's power as well as a younger leadership for panchayati raj. It also clearly demonstrated that democratic leaders from all political hues were not hesitant to declare their solidarity with him on this issue.

11

West Bengal Panchayat Polls of 1993

When Jyoti Basu completed sixteen years as the chief minister of West Bengal and became the politician with the longest term in power, next only to Jawaharlal Nehru, he had also acquired the distinction of being the only chief minister who had conducted four consecutive elections to panchayati raj institutions without fail. The panchayat elections of May-June 1993 in West Bengal should not just be seen as another feather in his cap but a lesson to the rest of the country as to the kind of rural and social transformation which can be brought about if village panchayats are treated as units of self-government, and the state governments adhere to the principle of grassroots-level democracy.

Strengthening Panchayats through Regular Elections

When 30 May 1993 was announced as the date for panchayat polls, it evoked a lot of interest in quarters concerned with decentralised governance. I could only gauge its significance for other countries experimenting in democratic forms when I received a message from Beijing that the department of basic level government, Ministry of Civil Affairs of the People's Republic of China, wished to send an "unofficial" six-member team, headed by its rural division chief, Wang Zhen Yao, to have a first-hand account of the entire electoral process in West Bengal including the campaign and polling arrangements. My visit to the West Bengal countryside during these elections, along with the Chinese team, was an eye-opener.

West Bengal has a three-tier panchayat system–gram panchayats, panchayat samitis, and zilla parishads. More than thirty million voters elect 71,119 members to these three levels–the gram panchayats have 61,010 seats, the panchayat samitis 9,453 seats, and the zilla parishads, 656 seats. Out of these, 1,903 members were elected without contest–1,710 at the Gram Panchayat, 191 at the Panchayat Samiti, and two at the Zilla Parishad level. In these elections for 69,216 positions, 224,110 candidates contested. The polling was over in just one day in the 37,677 polling booths, and had involved a total expense of eighteen crore rupees. The polling process had been manned and managed entirely by state officials on temporary duty. This statistical information is important to gauge the massive preparation needed to hold the elections within such a brief span of time–the elections were notified on 10 March and completed by 3 June.

Compare this with the Cambodian elections, which took place almost at the same time. In Cambodia 4.7 million voters took seven days to cast their votes and the expense involved was to the tune of forty million U.S. dollars. In West Bengal, without the use of computers or other means that can be called sophisticated, the officials did a magnificent job in managing and conducting the elections, because of their history of conducting regular panchayat elections. When democracy takes deep roots at the village level, elections become a way of life, a tradition. Once engrained, such traditions strengthen the observance of the rules of the game.

Dynamics of Democratic Politics

An analysis of the results shows that the elections were a reflection of people's assessment of a party which has been at the helm of affairs for several years. The Left Front got 65.5 percent of the seats, that is, 8 percent less than the previous panchayat elections but about 3.4 percent more than in 1983. The Congress(I) got 26.2 percent, which was 4.2 percent more than the previous total. But the Congress had bagged 32.2 percent seats in the 1983 elections.

The BJP made gains by securing 3.5 percent of the seats while in the previous elections it only had 0.86 percent seats. In absolute terms, the BJP has 125 seats in the panchayat samitis, while it had only three in the 1988 elections. At the Gram Panchayat level it got 2,366 seats when it had got only thirty-six previously. The BJP drew a blank in the zilla parishads. The popular view that the BJP is an urban-based party should change with these results. There has been a decline in the number of seats for the CPI(M) at all levels since the 1988 elections–5.5 percent at Gram Panchayat, 4.4 percent at Panchayat Samiti and a marginal 0.6 percent at the Zilla Parishad level. Data on votes polled by each party at all levels is not available yet. But according to unofficial computations the BJP has got about 4 percent of the votes at the Gram Panchayat level and 3 percent at the Panchayat Samiti level.

The BJP-Congress(I) alliance was an important issue in West Bengal this time. Covert understandings at the lower levels have been acknowledged by both parties. Joint sample ballot papers of the two parties were distributed at different places. The perception of these two parties that the CPI(M) is their common enemy is born of the popular belief that the enemy's enemy is a friend. In Kerala too the BJP-Congress understanding in elections came about from the very same political myopia. How short-sighted such alliances can turn out to be politically needs no explanation. The best example is the by-election to the border municipal town of Habra (with a population of 100,000 only), where the BJP could, for the first time, control a municipality in the state. The Congress(I) made this possible by withdrawing its fourteen candidates in the BJPs favour.

It was evident that the organisational weakness of the BJP and the Congress(I) in the rural areas made them rely on each other. It was also evident that the BJP used local issues to its advantage for its avowed philosophy of *hindutva* (resurgent Hindu nationalism). Ayodhya was kept for selective use but the refugees issue was cashed on. Infiltration from Bangladesh easily angers the village and town people in the border areas and because of this the BJP has been successful to a certain extent in its propaganda that the CPI(M) is closing its eyes to the refugees and consequently smuggling is thriving in these areas. The BJPs position has been that illegal immigration from a Muslim neighbouring state could also harm the cause of the Indian Muslims who are genuine citizens of the country. The panchayat pradhans are authorised to issue certificates which entitle the immigrants to obtain ration cards. The panchayat elections, therefore, become important. The BJP, which had no representative in the outgoing assembly, fielded candidates for forty thousand (52 percent) seats; among them 2,200 were from Muslim dominated areas.

A major reason for the decline in the Left Front's victory tally was the lack of unity and understanding among the alliance. According to reports, there were more than six thousand seats where the partners were fighting among themselves for supremacy, resulting in bickerings and unhealthy infights. Of course the people will get disillusioned!

The other factors leading to people's disenchantment with the Left have been instances of nepotism, corruption and political terror. It is common knowledge here that prosperity in certain hamlets comes only to the CPI(M) sympathisers. Projects like small irrigation networks or drinking water supply have not been completed, either because funds were squandered or due to political differences. A scandal broke out in Cooch Behar during these elections, following the news that the CPI(M) had misappropriated funds meant for literacy programmes. Elections are occasions when such omissions and commissions can be brought to light, discussed, debated (and sometimes even blown out of proportion). Only democracy at the grassroots level gives the opportunity for this wonderful churning process. The CPI(M), after having been in power for fifteen long years in these local self-government institutions, was naturally at the receiving end. If it escaped with minor bruises it speaks volumes for its rapport with the rural masses.

Prosperous Villages

The belief that panchayati raj and the CPI(M) have become coterminous in West Bengal has its roots in the fact that both have been complementary factors in the remarkable development that has taken place in the countryside. In 1943, Bengal experienced the most tragic famine deaths. Although official estimates put the death toll at 1.5 million, Amartya Sen, in *Poverty and Famines* (1986), has persuasively argued that the figure could cross three million. The state of West Bengal, which today is one-third of what it was in 1943, but with a population above sixty-seven million (1991), is showing signs of prosperity.

The contribution of the agricultural sector to the state income (at 1980-81 prices) has increased in a decade from 28.3 percent to 30 percent (1990-91) while in most other major states the share of agriculture in the total income has declined. In 1991-92 foodgrain production was 128.56 lakh tonnes of which 119.54 lakh tonnes was rice. There is a breakthrough in farm output. At the recorded level of 1991-92, West Bengal was the highest producer of rice in the country. The output of potatoes is another achievement. From 19.11 lakh tonnes in 1977-78 it has reached 49.43 lakh tonnes today. The output of fisheries and oilseeds production has also shown a significant increase. The key to the "green revolution" in West Bengal has been the poor farmer. According to government sources, the highest record production per hectare has been obtained from the lands of the poorer farmers.

The crucial role panchayats have played in giving the poorer farmer the capacity to produce through the effective implementation of the "land to the tiller" principle (Operation *Barga*) is now well known. Barga means share-cropping and a *bargadar* is a sharecropper. Till September 1991, 12.69 lakh acres of surplus land were in the possession of the government. Of this, 9.39 lakh acres were distributed to 20.48 lakh tenants (bargadars). Out of these the Scheduled Castes and Scheduled Tribes constituted 58 percent! This is no mean achievement in a region where landlords had ruled and zamindari had been the order of the day, even though it had been abolished on paper after independence. Many of the candidates we talked to were the beneficiaries of this radical measure, which would have been impossible without a vibrant panchayat system. The local bodies have taken up minor irrigation projects in a big way, thus helping the entire process.

A blot on the village development process are the disparities that exist at the lowest levels. Take the case of agricultural labour. The average wage of a male agricultural labourer in Cooch Behar is 17.10 rupees but in South Parganas it goes up to 27.10 rupees. In Burdwan it is 20.25 rupees. The candidates of the CPI(M) are aware of this gap. When we asked a CPI(M) candidate who belonged to the lowest strata what her priority would be if she were to be elected, she said that she would work to get equal wages for all farm labourers.

Administrative Tensions

The interface between the bureaucracy and the elected representatives at the panchayat level is going to be a serious problem in the days to come. Their equation could make or mar these local institutions. In the words of B. D. Ghosh, director, State Institute of Panchayats, West Bengal, "The panchayati raj institutions have little chance of success unless they can exercise control over the well-entrenched district bureaucracy" (1993: 6). What one could witness in West Bengal is the development, over the years, of a satisfactory working arrangement between the state officials and people's representatives.

In West Bengal, when the district magistrate was brought under the control of the Zilla Parishad as its executive officer, the message conveyed was that the Zilla Parishad and its chairperson cannot be taken lightly by the bureaucracy. Moreover, the district officers at the Zilla Parishad level were made members of various standing committees *(sthayee samitis).* But the crucial question has been the attitudinal change in the bureaucracy. How did West Bengal's panchayats bring this about? It could not have been possible but for the launching of imaginative and sustained programmes to encourage the interface between the disadvantaged people and the officials. For instance, when pro-poor development in the villages became the main thrust of the panchayati raj institutions through Operation Barga, a unique programme was undertaken by the West Bengal government to bring about this attitudinal change. In the words of D. Bandyopadhyay, who, as secretary of rural development, played a vital role in the implementation of Operation Barga:

> The government has undertaken a programme of holding reorientation camps where thirty to forty landless agricultural labourers and sharecroppers and a dozen or two officers of different ranks stay together, eat together and work together for three to four days. The village poor are encouraged to speak out their bitterness....Having seen their own images in the eyes of the poor quite a few officials felt disturbed and started questioning the correctness of their past behaviour and activities. It sets in a process of change of mind at least among a few functionaries at the cutting edges of the administration (1991).

In West Bengal now both the officials and elected representatives have come to recognise that one cannot do without the other. The primacy is for the elected representatives because the underlying principle involved is the sovereignty of the people.

An Irreversible Trend

Travelling through the countryside of West Bengal during the run up to the panchayat elections, one thing was most discernible. Panchayats have taken firmer roots in the state. A Bengali villager cannot now imagine his life without the panchayats. The parliament, the assembly, even the district parishads are far away in his scheme of things. But the Gram Panchayat and the Panchayat Samiti at the block level are day to day realities; much of the villagers' life revolves around these democratic institutions. So he has a stake in the elections, which come every five years. It also explains the high percentage of polling. In the polls of 1993 more than 75 percent of the voters cast their votes.

The graffiti, the flags, the wall posters which enliven the dusty village roads, houses or tea shops, convey not only a message but also a lot of meaning about democracy and the democratic process in a multi-party setting. If a visitor asks a candidate of the opposition party whether the previous panchayat has done any good to the village, his/her answer is positive and catalogues a series of developmental work done. Why then oppose? The answer is, things could be better. That is the spirit of democracy at the grassroots level.

The Chinese delegation was asked what was the most impressive aspect of the elections witnessed by them in West Bengal. Their reply was: enthusiastic women's participation, the large number of women candidates, the smooth management of elections and the self-imposed discipline of citizens at the booths. What was the negative aspect? Of course, the election-related violence. (The official figure for panchayat poll-related killings were forty-two deaths.) From the perspective of their own political system, it was difficult for the Chinese to fully appreciate the separation of state officials from the party/multi-party contests, or the vigorous campaigning and stiff competitiveness of the elections.

In an exchange of views on panchayats with the Chinese delegation, Chief Minister Jyoti Basu emphasized that though he was proud of all the achievements of the panchayati raj institutions he was also concerned at not being able to effectively tackle illiteracy in the villages. Today, West Bengal ranks only sixth among the Indian states in terms of literacy (57.70 percent). He told us that in the next five years attention will be focussed on the education of the rural masses through panchayats. What the *Sastra Sahitya Parishad* had achieved in Kerala, could also effectively, and on a more sustained basis, be done in West Bengal through panchayati raj institutions.

12

The Chinese Experiment With Local Self-Government

I

"Self-government in villages is a great democratic movement in China. Over the past three years our province has implemented it in a conscious manner. Village self-government means people are masters of their homeland," said Zhang Zhi Xin, vice-director of Lioning Provincial Civil Department. What China presents today in its villages, in terms of their attempts to govern themselves, attracts attention because of its determined effort to give power to the people notwithstanding the central role of the Communist party.

Lioning Province (40 million people), in northeast China, is an industrially developed area. Shenyang, its capital, is one of the biggest cities in the country with a population touching six million. During our more than one-week's stay in the province we had about ten meetings in the different villages with the elected representatives of the villagers' committees, and a few with district and county officials. Most of the villages were far into the interior. Our programme also included visits to homes and discussions with members of the households. In the meetings with the villagers' committees, the chief (that is, the director or chairman) would give a presentation about the village, its work and achievements and then the visiting team

The author was in China in 1992 along with an eight member team from the U.S.A., U.K., Japan, Indonesia, Philippines and Bangladesh, at the invitation of the ministry of civil affairs of the People's Republic of China. The team visited numerous Chinese villages to study the Chinese experiment with local self-government (which included the election process), and also participated in an international seminar with Chinese official representatives in Beijing in July 1992. He was again in China in August 1993, to study villager's committees in Jilin Province and to participate in another international seminar, held in Beijing on Villagers' Committees in China.

would engage him in discussions lasting two to three hours. These often turned out to be "grilling sessions."

The Organic Law of the Villagers' Committees

The Chinese village self-government system is based on the Organic Law of the Villagers' Committees which was adopted for trial implementation in November 1987 by the National People's Congress Standing Committee. This is the fundamental law of the grassroots organisation in the countryside. It may be recalled here that after the 1949 revolution the rural organisations underwent three changes. The first change took place between 1949 to 1956. During this period, the Chinese Communist party led the people from a new democratic set up to socialism. This period saw the establishment of township political power and agricultural producers cooperatives. The second stage was from 1958 to 1982, involving the people's communes. People's communes, production brigades and production teams were the primary organisations in the countryside. The communes were turned into revolutionary committees of the production brigade during the Cultural Revolution. The third change was in December 1982 with the adoption of the new constitution by the National People's Congress. A new era of opening up of China's economy had begun. The villagers' committee became the primary mass organisations in the countryside.

When the twenty-four year old production brigade was dissolved, the farmers began to spontaneously set up mass organisations of the villagers' committees to sustain social security, to mediate disputes and to manage public affairs. This system was formally accepted in the new constitution.

The system of government in China has four levels: the central, the provincial, the county and the township level. The township level government is the lowermost extension of state power in the countryside. The villagers' committee, elected directly by all villagers above eighteen years, for a period of three years, is the primary mass organisation of self-government in which villagers manage their own affairs, educate themselves and serve their own needs. It consists of the chief, the deputy chief and three to seven members and is established in a natural village. For example, Xiao Yangan, an average village on the outskirts of Shenyang city, consists of 387 households, 1,449 inhabitants and 241.8 hectares (1 ha = 2.471 acres) of farm fields. In some cases, two or more small natural villages may jointly establish a villagers' committee. Under the new law, two elections have been held so far to the villagers' committees, in 1988 and 1991 respectively. Serious thought is now being given to extend the term of the committees from three to five years. In 1991 China had 1,018,593 villagers' committees. (Incidentally, India has about 206,264 village panchayats.)

China's local government also has villagers' meetings (similar to our Grama Sabha) consisting of all persons above eighteen years. Decisions are taken by a majority of the members or a majority of household representatives. Wherever the population is large and scattered, villagers' conferences are set up comprising elected representatives selected on the basis of one representative for every ten families for a period of three years. The villagers' meeting has the right to recall the members of the villagers' committees.

The buildings which house the villagers' committees are impressive, spacious enough to become the nerve-centre of village activities. Special space is provided to notify the budgets and accounts of expenditure in detail, the progress made in the projects, and so on. Public accountability is ensured with the maximum care. These buildings, constructed in the last ten years or so, are maintained fairly well; some of the buildings are adorned by a row of portraits: Marx, Engels, Lenin, Sun-Yat-Sen and Mao, in that order. While visiting these villagers' committee buildings, I felt ashamed of the state of neglect of our panchayat buildings in most states.

The financial position of these villagers' committees is on a firm footing. They generate their own resources and give 1.2 percent from these to the township government. This "bottom-upwards" financial arrangement for local governments in China is possible because even today there is no private ownership of land. Under the new dispensation, the land is contracted to families for agriculture and the farmers, in return, have to give a part of their income to the villagers' committees. In addition, they have income from village enterprises (some are private), orchards, fishing tanks and special grants from the provincial government. What a contrast to the situation prevailing in our country where the local bodies are starved and wait to be fed from above!

The key to the success of the present villagers' committees is the radical land reform China implemented. It seems that in developing agricultural societies, whenever land reforms have been implemented, the local-level governments have proved to be a success. In our country, West Bengal is a case in point.

China Lives in the Villages

In our meetings with the village representatives, I often found myself asking, "What is the ultimate goal of your village self-government? Is it to achieve maximum production?" The answer was a surprising no. The aim was to achieve a comfortable life for all people. As the vice-mayor of a county we visited put it, "Chinese farmers have been preoccupied with hard work to earn their bread; now they are concentrating their attention on village democracy and autonomy in order to raise their physical and 'spiritual' quality of life."

But this has become complicated today because when basic needs are fulfilled, people aim for more; their needs also change. Then the question that arises is how to satisfy these changing needs. Especially when China is opening its door to a capitalist form of development and welcoming multinationals and foreign investors with open arms, the borderline between the present egalitarian situation existing in the villages and the unequal, competitive, greed-oriented and exploitative society seems very thin. China is faster on economic reform than on political reform. The numerous official banquets hosted for us by mayors, vice-mayors and other dignitaries in various places ended with the plea to "please invest in our area. Tell your friends that we shall provide everything necessary."

Visiting Chinese villages reminds one of the popularly held belief that China lives in its villages. I was reminded of how the rulers of our country betrayed Gandhiji's dream of India living in its villages. Our leaders remember India's villages only in homilies and in official declarations that there is no programme "more important or urgent than rural development" as far as India is concerned. The result: even in 1992 there are people in our land who live by eating only rats, without ever having tasted a full meal.

The seminar in Beijing with government officials, academics and people's representatives was the first of its kind, as earlier, political questions were never discussed and criticism never entertained in the company of foreign visitors. Democracy at the village level as understood in China, which is totally different from what we have here in India or anywhere else where the Westminster model is followed, was one major point of debate. Whenever our criticism tended to cross tolerable limits, the Chinese friends used to gently remind us that considering the history of autocracy and of the feudal system China had inherited, the change to the present village democracy based on equity was unique.

In our discussions with the district, county and villagers' committee officials and elected leaders, they admitted that there were several shortcomings in their system. It was refreshing to hear that they were open to suggestions and criticism from us. At another level when we returned to Beijing we had a free and frank exchange of views on our field exposure with government officials, political personalities, academicians and county level representatives. If this openness is taken to its logical end, China's village government system will spring surprises for the rest of the world, specially its model of grassroots level democracy.

Competitive politics works in a limited way in China. In almost all villages visited by us we were told that there was a consensus about the candidates and only very few persons contested for the seats in the villagers' committees. Even then, they were finding the processing of nominations and the procedures connected with it the single-most pressing problem. This kind of elections remind one of "consensus politics" with all its negative aspects. They are akin to the *Sarvodaya* (a movement for the uplift of all) idea that there should be consensus in village affairs, and party politics should not enter village panchayat elections. But one could feel that this kind of "limited competitive politics" had marred the real spirit of democracy in China, preventing people's participation either as candidates or as enthusiastic voters.

Role of the Communist Party

In a way, musclemen, money-power, caste and other dominating factors which bring about consensus in the Indian situation are replaced with the Communist party domination in the "consensus elections" at the village level. Only one or two non-party persons are elected as members to the villagers' committees. And in most cases the party secretary and the chairman of the villagers' committee will be the same person. In the course of the many discussions, I asked them why they could not implement the one post for one person principle. A general quest to loosen the grip of the party to allow at least 50 percent of the members to be from a non-party background is in evidence.

The liberal Chinese political opinion about the party is that in future it should guide but not dominate. They believe that the role of the party is limited but not unlimited. An opinion is gaining ground that the party is not omnipotent. But orthodox thinking still insists that the party should lead in everything. The party cadres seem to be wary of democracy. Their reasoning seems to be that the Western type of democracy will bring chaos instead of stability. On the other hand, Chinese scholars and functionaries who advocate further liberalisation in politics reply that democracy will contribute to stability if it is handled well.

Another point which raises doubts about the "democratic" elections is that the same villagers' committees were being elected again and again, with minor changes or with no changes at all. In a couple of cases, the previous chairpersons are now the ordinary members. In the early stages of the Chinese election process this latter fact itself was found to be a radical break.

Status of Women

Regarding the status of women, Chinese society has a long way to go. There is no reservation for women in elected bodies. In the villagers' committees there were just one or two women representatives and it was in most cases a goodwill gesture towards them and not a matter of their right, barring a few cases in which women were important functionaries of the party. We did not come across a single woman chairperson of the villagers' committees. But as in India, individual cases of women reaching positions of power are not rare. The vice-chairperson of the standing committee of Lioning Province, Chen Suzhi, is an outstanding leader in her sixties. She was formerly a governor of the province. In the reception hosted by her we were told that Suzhi began her career in a machine factory and in 1977 came to the provincial government as the in-charge of industry and transportation.

It is generally felt that there is a gulf between theory and practice in the matter of women's equality. In the elections, at some levels, there is only one vote for one household and it goes without saying that this vote is exercised by a male member of the household. In most villagers' committees, the woman member handles women's welfare, family planning and allied subjects. At the same time it must be said to the credit of these few women representatives in the committees that they are articulate, bold and with a lot of leadership qualities. They read more than one newspaper, magazine or weekly, and they are aware of the developments in their township, county, province and the nation. Women's literacy in China is on par with that of men's. Most of them have read up to the sixth or seventh class.

Younger leadership is coming to the fore in China at the village level. The villagers' committee's youngest member's average age is twenty-five years. Most of the representatives are in the thirty-five to forty-five age group.

The question of corruption at the village level was rather puzzling. To repeated questions regarding the checks and balances to curb the possibilities of corruption and nepotism, the standard answer was that there was no corruption, and so on. It must be said that hitherto the chances of corruption have been minimal because of the regimented economic control but it cannot be said with certainty that this will be the case after liberalisation. Party leadership at the local levels becoming a source of corruption through the contracts and the market economy is a reality that cannot be ruled out.

Mao's Vision and Gandhiji's Philosophy

But in spite of all these, after the villagers' committees came into being, production increased, the per capita income of the farmers went up, the infrastructural developments were speedier and there was a general sense of participation from the people.

In the case of an average village like Xiao Yangan, the total output value has increased from 0.42 million yuan in 1982 to forty-five million yuan in 1991. Its per capita income has gone up from 156 to 1,350 yuan. It has twenty-two enterprises and two orchards. The village invested 0.45 million yuan to install a drinking water system, to repair the primary school building, renovate the village road and install a telephone exchange. The neighbouring Qianmiu village, in addition, has supplies of liquefied gas, pension for all above sixty, a new basketball field, an entertainment centre and a library-cum-reading room. This is just a pointer to what people can do when they have power.

New institutions have come up along with small industries, related to agriculture and locally available mineral resources. One such institution run in a remote village, a nursery, attracted our attention because of its exemplary management, excellent atmosphere for the children and high standards of pre-school education. Parents pay fifteen yuan per month per child sent to the nursery, which is extremely cheap for the kind of care they get during the day, when both the parents are at work.

From the political angle skeptics continue to ask: Is village self-government a beginning for democratising the entire Chinese system from the bottom upwards or a convenient ploy to contain the democratic urge at the lower, safer levels? To the Western scholars, it seems paradoxical to find decentralisation and local self-government functioning alongside a strong centralised system.

But ground realities have so far shown that the villagers' committee system, with all the trappings of one-party rule, may be a small beginning in terms of democratisation but politically it is a significant step.

Chaudhury Charan Singh, in his book, *Economic nightmare of India: Its cause and cure* (perhaps a forgotten book by now) in 1981, had made a pertinent observation that if in China people are better fed and clothed than the people in India, one of the reasons is that China has taken more than a leaf from Gandhiji's teachings. Charan Singh was right. Mao Zedong had given priority to agriculture and had relied generally on human labour and decentralised labour-intensive enterprises. And thus China has proved correct the famous saying of Gandhiji that "the earth provides enough to satisfy every man's needs, but not for every man's greed." The villagers' committee system, if implemented in its true democratic spirit, has the potential to take Mao's vision and Gandhiji's philosophy forward to the twenty-first century.

July 1992

II

"We are keen to bring about democracy in China. We have a long way to go. In this the most important factor is elections to the villagers' committees," observed Hou'an Zhang, well known professor at the Institute of Scientific Socialism, Wuhan Central China Teachers University, during the international meet in Beijing in August 1993, convened to review the working of villagers' committees in China. Professor Zhang's statement is significant in view of the question being asked these days as to whether China is at the threshold of democracy or not.

This second visit to China has convinced me that at the lower level China is opening up not only on the economic but also on the political front. When Chinese economic reforms are in full throttle, can political opening be far behind? The banner at the Beijing international airport and the writings all over the city walls saying "A more open China awaits 2000 Olympics" were symbolic of this trend. Of course, now it is the 2004 Olympics that await a more open China, but that is another matter!

Step for Democracy

As one can perceive now, the villagers' committees will be the foundation of the future of China's democracy. China's reforms in the countryside began at the end of 1978 when the contract system started developing. Each household could contract agricultural land for cultivation after paying a certain levy to the township government. The farmer could earn from what he produced. That was the beginning of higher production as well as economic reform. Once this happened in the Chinese villages, reforms in the administrative system were inevitable.

The Chinese Communist Party's Central Committee of June 1981 took an important decision to "gradually realise direct participation of the people in the democratic process at the grassroots of political power and community life." This, of course, was aimed at the fundamental task of establishing a highly democratic, socialist political system. As a result the Chinese Constitution of 1982 stipulated that villagers' committees established among rural residents were the "mass organisations of self-government at the grassroots level." This was a watershed in China's long march towards village democracy. But the interesting thing to be noted here is that as soon as remuneration was linked to output in the contract system, farmers began to spontaneously form self-government organisations. They did not wait for constitutional sanction. Zhending County in Hebei Province was the first to give expression to the people's urge by establishing villagers' committees.

While this resulted in radical changes in the rural economy and in social relations, the lowest tier of government still stopped at the township. A township in China has fifteen to twenty villages. In 1983 the township government administration was separated from the economic management of villagers' committees. The townships were to work out regulations for the villagers' committees, according to local situations. The aim was to evolve nationwide organic regulations for this new village system. The twenty-third meeting of the Standing Committee of the Sixth National People's Congress adopted the Organic Law of the Villagers' Committees, which began to be implemented from June 1988.

Today, except Guangdong, Hainan, Jiangxi and Yunnan (provinces), Guanxi, Tibet (autonomous regions), Beijing and Shanghai (municipalities), the remaining twenty-two provinces in China have adopted the regulations regarding the villagers' committees.

The period of legalised democracy in China since 1978 was an open admission that class struggle was no longer relevant as a means to solve political and social problems. This was a quantum jump from the highly centralised democracy of pre-1949 China or the "mass mobilisation" democracy with characteristics of military communism which China experienced between 1949 and 1978.

The Election Process

This year I visited Jilin Province in the northeast (capital: Changchun; population: 24,600,000 of which 14,600,000 rural) to study the election process of the villagers' committees. Most of my time was spent in Lishu County which is an experimental county for implementing villagers' committees. Jilin has a sizeable number of Korean and Muslim minorities but there are no majority-minority tensions in this province. For that matter, one can say that China is almost free from this problem.

China's rural population of nine hundred million has no tradition of democracy at all. In the past township and village officials used to be elected by a show of hands or by putting beans in a bowl. The mentality of attaching importance to the ballot system, or to elected office with a fixed tenure, was non-existent. But today villagers have begun to attach importance to the ballot. Election verdicts are respected. In the 1993 local government elections, many people holding high offices were voted out, including the governors of the provinces. The central government respected the verdict, and made no changes, something which was unimaginable before. "If the historical background, with the absence of legalised democracy in rural China for the past several thousand years, is taken into consideration, the strides made in the elections to villagers' committees in recent years are tremendous," said an official of the Jilin Province.

Since 1988 there are direct elections for the posts of chairman, vice chairman and members of the villagers' committees. The Chinese law says that a candidate must get a minimum of 50 percent of the total votes in the village to get elected. There were several villages where positions were vacant because the contestants could not make it. What is the criteria on which villagers cast their votes wherever elections are held on a competitive basis, I wondered? The discussion I had at Niuxinding Township was revealing. Portraits of Marx, Engels, Lenin and Stalin adorned the meeting room. This township, which has 12,944 people, 3,251 households, 35,848 *mu* (1 mu = 1/6 acre) of arable land and fifty-nine village community groups, has eight villagers' committees with chairpersons, vice-chairpersons and five members each. Each village has an assembly too with 184 members.

In one of these village assemblies there were fifty women members. And only fifty-six were party members. Yu Shuxian (39) was the head of his village, Xiaohebei, in 1989-92. She was hardworking, bold in taking decisions regarding reforms, had promoted village enterprises (one such was a wine factory) and when the area was affected by floods, she had gone there personally and worked with the people. She also implemented state policies meticulously. In the 1992 elections she was voted to the township level.

Yu Shuxian may be an exception. By and large women's representation is very poor. At the People's Congress and the Party Congress, 20 percent of the seats are reserved for women and there is an all-round demand for accepting this norm in basic level democracies too. India's constitutional amendment to give one-third elected positions to women in panchayati raj institutions was regarded as a great step by Chinese scholars and officials.

In Xinyua village, at the outskirts of Changhun city, I was told by villagers that they voted for people who gave them guidance to become rich first! After the villagers' committees came into being this area had acquired better roads, thirteen village enterprises, better quality modern houses and, above all, pension schemes for the elderly.

Men above sixty-five years get sixty yuan per month and women above sixty get 100 yuan. The most beautiful and best building in the area is the school building. Children are provided the best possible conditions for education. The township also has an old age home–the elder-friendly complex with a Chinese name, Rural Palace of the Township. There are nine joint ventures in collaboration with the U.S.A., Japan, Taiwan, Australia, Hongkong and South Korea.

An election process typical to Niuxinding village, as described by the officials and elected members, was very revealing. Elections take place under the guidance of the party. It may be pointed out here that there is no distinction between government officials and party functionaries in China, unlike in India. The "officials" at the township level organise the elections and look after the arrangements. One month before the elections all adults (above 18 years) are registered as voters. Then begins the identification of candidates. Ten to fifteen households discuss among themselves who should be the candidate. This is the sub-group. It submits names to the larger body–the village group. After the latters approval, the names go to the villagers' assembly. The villagers' assembly scrutinises the list and may send it back to the village group or sub-group for re-examination in case questions are raised about the nominated persons or if the number of candidates at the preliminary stage is very large. The number of candidates must be limited to near consensus level. Finally, the names approved by the assembly are published five days before the elections. It is difficult for a citizen to offer his candidature on his own–although the author was told this happens in some places. Each name must be cleared from sub-group to village group to village assembly level.

In the discussions in Lishu County it was clear that in spite of holding two elections since 1988, my Chinese hosts could not say that they had achieved a satisfactory election system. There were several reasons for this state of affairs. The party cadres feared that people may not exercise their franchise with responsibility because of their low political consciousness, therefore resulting in disorder. Another argument was that able persons may not always get elected in elections and those getting elected may not bring forth bold reforms for fear of the people's anger or displeasure. The ordinary villagers also contribute to the overall skepticism regarding elections. They think that direct elections are a farce or a ritual because ultimately those in higher positions will have their way. Moreover some village communities in China resist having to adapt to the changing reality of democratic governance.

One can observe that regulations pertaining to elections are not strictly enforced in many areas. It may be mentioned here that there are no uniform regulations on the election of villagers' committees within the country or even within a province. Only in very rare cases and in few counties do election campaigns take place. These campaigns are limited to public speeches or to announcing plans for governing the village. Of course, these are nowhere near the campaign or election fever we experience in our panchayat or municipal elections. Another astonishing aspect is that there is no secrecy of vote in the Chinese elections. There also are villages and townships where people hesitate to come forward to contest elections. The director of civil affairs, Jilin Province, in his meeting with me confessed, "In a country with a long feudal history, full competitive elections are not easy. It takes time. In Lishu County we encouraged people to come forward to contest but it was not very successful." This is the case in many parts of China. A typical election day finds villagers assembling, marking the ballot papers in the hall or in open spaces.

In order to overcome the present inertia among the people regarding elections, the China Research Society for Basic Level Governance and the department of basic-level governance under the ministry of civil affairs have massive programmes to conduct studies for villagers on the provisions of the organic law, the door to door campaign, as well as training courses for government officials.

In the international conference in Beijing all the five top officials from the Chinese government present were the same persons who had been to West Bengal to study the panchayat elections held on 30 May 1993. They were all praise for the conduct of elections in India and declared: "Nobody among us really knew what a secret ballot was until we went to India and saw the voting procedure for ourselves." Their concern was that they wanted to bring about "genuine" elections and through that, genuine democracy, and this they will have to learn from other countries. "We fervently hope that we will be able to learn from the other's experiences," was the constant refrain at the conference. Chinese officials consider India's experience with democracy very important for China to learn from. Whatever may be the election method and election process, the achievements of the villagers' committees are spoken of with pride by both officials and representatives.

Economic Prosperity and Market Reforms

The story of a farmer in Niuxinding, belonging to the Manchu minority community, is representative of the new economic prosperity in the interior northeastern regions. He has a chicken farm with six thousand birds, a well constructed house and a farm measuring eleven mu. It has been contracted for fifteen years. He has to pay twenty-five yuan per mu per year to the township government and forty yuan as contribution to the villagers' committee for the entire area. The rate is fixed by the villagers' committee and the assembly according to the guidelines set by the township government. His house cost him seven thousand yuan for which he had taken a two thousand yuan loan from the bank at 10.9 percent interest. He has two school-going daughters aged fourteen and seven. He wants to educate them as much as he can. He has acquired a television recently. The average per capita income per farmer in China is 1,100 yuan. In one ordinary village it was found that the income before 1988 was just six hundred yuan per capita but today, after the villagers' committees have come into being, the income has increased to eight hundred yuan. The households are going for better houses, consumer durables, and education for their children. The houses are built under cooperatives. It is evident that China is moving from state socialism to people's cooperatives.

What is really happening in China is that the country is transforming its planned economy to a socialist market economy. According to the statistics released by Yang Zhong, deputy director of the leading group for economic development of impoverished areas under the state council, the poor people have decreased from 250 million in 1978 to eighty million in 1992. The author was given this information during this latest visit. Poor people, who did not have enough food and clothing in the rural areas, made up 31.3 percent of the total rural population in 1978. But in 1992 this average had come down to 8.8 percent. Chinese authorities are now saying that the opportunities brought in by the market economy must be grasped by the people in these backward rural areas.

The officials and party cadres are guarded against the increasing corruption in the government and the party and the consequent dissatisfaction among the peasants. Chairman Deng Xiao Ping used to philosophise by saying, "When we open our windows some flies will get in." This is all the more true of China's present experience. But the intellectuals are worried and openly talk about it, maintaining that only more democracy could counter these "flies." Chinese scholars claim that what is happening in their villages is "basic level democracy with

Chinese characteristics." What is in store at various levels may only be "democracy with Chinese characteristics."

"Democracy at the basic-level government in the countryside cannot be separated from the democracy within the party, in the country and in society. What is happening in the villagers' committees is part of the systematic movement for democracy. These two aspects are complementary," declared professor Haiuan Zhang while bidding me farewell. This indicates the conviction with which all those concerned with the future of democracy in China are working.

August 1993

Part Four

Politics and the Panchayats

13

The Congress(I)

The drawbacks and shortcomings of panchayati raj have been blown out of all proportion by the protagonists of centralised administration and by power-peddlers. These shortcomings stemmed essentially from a socio-political problem which could have been tackled to a great extent by holding regular elections and by allowing the political process to take its logical course. The resulting political education of communities which had been exploited for ages would have certainly changed the scenario. When elections are held regularly in rural areas, there are various permutations and combinations, with traditional rivalries disappearing and issue-oriented groupings emerging. Wherever this process was allowed full play, there were not infrequent cases of a *dhobi* (washerman) or a barber getting elected to positions till then monopolised by a particular caste or a family. This change of power equations is not a small matter in our traditional society. Simple mechanical solidarity begins to give way to more organic solidarity and individual freedom of opinion and group positions emerge. But it is precisely this transformation that was feared by the ruling elites, and the Congress party, which held power, arrested this healthy development.

In the National Development Council meeting held in 1988, the late prime minister, Rajiv Gandhi, had called for regular and periodical elections to the local bodies so that grassroots democracy could thrive along with grassroots planning. Elected local bodies, he had said, were indispensable for effective development at the local level. In one of the meetings of the Congress(I) Working Committee he had also directed all the Congress(I)-ruled states to hold elections to local bodies without further delay. The state governments were reminded that it was mandatory to hold elections to the panchayats and other local bodies on a regular basis. But the catch was that no definite time limit was set for completing these elections.

There was no dearth of official pronouncements or recommendations of government-appointed commissions about the necessity of holding regular elections and the vital role these institutions play in our polity. The L.M. Singhvi committee's draft concept paper on revitalisation of panchayati raj institutions for democracy and development, submitted to the ministry of agriculture in November 1986, had stated in unequivocal terms that local self-government should be constitutionally recognised, protected and preserved by the inclusion of a new chapter in the constitution. The committee wanted the government to constitutionally incorporate the panchayati raj institutions as the third tier of governance. The latest among these recommendations was that of the Sarkaria Commission for the strengthening of local bodies financially and functionally (Article 177 of the report of the Sarkaria Commission 1988). "Regular elections and sessions of these institutions is a must, and means for ensuring the same in all the states uniformly should be evolved" (Sarkaria Commission 1988). The commission also forwarded a request to incorporate the articles analogous to Articles 172 and 174 in the constitution. In spite of the plethora of official recommendations and despite the pronouncements of the top leadership, why were the Congress(I) governments indifferent to local elections?

Gujarat was the lone Congress(I)-ruled state where local elections had been held regularly. Even Maharashtra's good track record was marred by its successive decision to postpone these polls. The citizens of Delhi were deprived of elections to the Delhi Municipal Corporation and the Delhi Metropolitan Council, since these were postponed again and again till 1993. Civic elections in Uttar Pradesh, were held in 1971, seventeen years prior to the elections of 5 June 1988! In Rajasthan, where Jawaharlal Nehru inaugurated the first panchayati raj of independent India, calling it "the most revolutionary and historical step," the last elections in fifteen major towns were also held in 1971! In Orissa, under Congress rule, the situation was still worse. Out of one hundred civic bodies (27 municipalities and 73 notified area councils) six municipalities were superseded, five suspended, and in fourteen municipalities and notified area councils elections had not been held since the inception of the local bodies!

The states ruled by opposition parties are developing a pattern. As soon as they dislodge the Congress(I) from power in the state they hold the overdue elections. Elections were held in 1978 by the Left Front in West Bengal, in 1987 by the Janata in Karnataka, in 1987 by the Lok Dal in Haryana, in 1987 by the Left Democratic Front (LDF) in Kerala, in 1987 by the Telugu Desam in Andhra Pradesh and in 1992 by the Janata Dal in Orissa. The ruling parties were not the losers. Then why does the Congress(I), wherever it is the ruling party, get nervous at the very mention of local elections?

In fact, even when the Congress party is in the opposition it gains in such local elections. In Kerala, when the United Democratic Front (UDF) was dislodged from power in 1987, the rank and file of the Congress(I) was demoralised. But in the local elections, promptly ordered by the LDF, the Congress(I) and its allies bounced back. But why did the Congress(I) not conduct elections in Kerala in 1984, as scheduled, when it was in power? In Karnataka, too, the Congress(I), as the opposition party, gave a good fight to the Janata in Zilla Parishad and Mandal Panchayat elections by capturing 44.4 percent and 37.8 percent seats respectively. In the Mandal Zilla Parishad elections in Andhra Pradesh in 1987, the Congress(I), as in Kerala, hit back by putting up an impressive performance.

It has been proved that all political parties, whether cadre-based like the CPI(M), or non-cadre based, like the Congress or Janata, benefit from local elections because the electoral process revitalises the party machinery in villages, towns and cities. The best example is West Bengal. The impressive showing of the LDF, in spite of its internal bickerings, in the just-concluded local bodies elections of May 1993 was due to its having held such elections regularly since 1978. This has instilled confidence in the people that their grassroots-level bodies were being taken seriously by the state leadership.

When the party machinery at the state level is aware that regular elections will be held in the local bodies, it has to nurture leadership from the village upwards. Thus the panchayats, municipalities and corporations become nurseries of political leadership. Do the state and central-level political leaders deem these nurseries to be a potential threat to their dominance and existence? If they do, and for this reason thwart local elections on one pretext or the other, they are axing the vital institutions on which democracy rests. In Karnataka, when the national parties had to contest the local elections on party lines, it was hard for them to find a sufficient number of candidates at the village and district levels. In the present form of democracy, political parties are inevitable and if we destroy the base, how will these parties grow?

The poor can share power only if grassroots-level democracy is functional. If we throttle this avenue, our democracy will be further emasculated. One of the reasons for the pervading cynicism in the countryside is the lack of avenues for the poor to share the fruits of development. These avenues are more or less closed, if not eliminated, through the freezing of local bodies.

Karnataka saw local bodies bouncing to new life and assuming greater responsibilities under the Janata dispensation because of panchayati raj institutions not merely being made development agencies but also political units with considerable powers. The mandal panchayats were vying with one another to give utmost priority to primary education. Their target was a hundred percent increase in education. The attendance of teachers and students in schools had already shown remarkable improvement. The management of drinking water assets, improvement of health and rural communications were other areas voluntarily selected by the mandals for immediate attention.

Both Abdul Nazir Sab and Hegde had stated that after the new zilla parishads and mandals came into being the self-confidence and pride of the representatives increased to the extent that they were able to now demand papers and files from executive engineers and senior officers in the bureaucracy. People had begun to get the feeling that they were the rulers. This was the political dimension of the new wave of local self-government, not only in Karnataka, but also in Andhra Pradesh, West Bengal and Kerala. Our political leadership must give up its present philosophy of expediency. Who wins or loses in a local election is a small matter in the context of the long-term interests of the nation. Any ruling party which holds regular elections to local bodies and gives the importance due to them stands to gain.

All those concerned with panchayati raj had been pleading for a specific constitutional provision so that panchayati raj institutions could be invigorated by regular elections. But the Congress(I) was consistently backing out from this.

Whether in the realm of the economy or in the sphere of power, in order to transform their lives our people want to be "subjects" and not "objects" of mercy from above. The L.M. Singhvi committee's concept paper on panchayati raj institutions has correctly observed that these institutions should be organised as part of the process of democratic decentralisation in order to build up the institutional edifice from the grassroots upwards and not as a *gift* of the devolutionary process. Ramakrishna Hegde had observed, in the same vein, that no favour was being done to the people by giving back certain powers to them. He added that one tends to forget that power belongs to the people.

It was against this background that the Congress(I) government's much trumpeted 64th Constitution Amendment Bill to confer statutory status on panchayati raj was introduced in parliament on 15 May 1989. The bill, introduced without due spadework, raised the issue of federalism as a prerequisite for decentralisation of power.

The Congress(I) had two basic compulsions for introducing the ill-fated bill. First, in West Bengal, Karnataka and Andhra Pradesh, there had been a perceptible impact on the lives of the people due to the functioning of the second generation of panchayati raj. The Congress(I) leadership at the centre began to recognise the growing popularity of the non-Congress(I) governments in these states, besides the attention the latter received nationally for making devolution of power a practical proposition. Most of the Congress(I) state governments, on the other hand, were the objects of censure for keeping the local bodies in hibernation, either by not holding elections for decades altogether, or by superseding elected bodies and putting the grassroots level organisations under the charge of civil servants. So, with a view to retrieving lost ground with the electorate, the Rajiv Gandhi government suddenly hit on the idea of the panchayati raj bill.

Second, at least a few at the helm of affairs in the Congress(I) began to realise the evils and ramifications of concentration of power. The political and social implications of centralised power were becoming transparently debilitating. The cup was nearly full. On the economic front, for instance, Rajiv Gandhi had to admit that of every rupee earmarked for development, only fifteen paise reached the target group. Without proper functioning of the local bodies the growing frustration among the people could not be stemmed. But the Congress(I) sponsored constitution amendment bill, drafted and introduced in haste had, sadly, missed the wood for the trees.

II

On the heels of panchayati raj becoming a part of our constitution in 1993, the Congress(I), the biggest political party in the country, planned a two-day meet at Amethi on the theme of panchayati raj. This was a welcome development. After all, without the support of a political party like the Congress, the institutions of self-government which are intended to give power to the people and a new meaning to grassroots-level democracy, will not be successful. It is a sad *denouement* that nature's fury struck at the venue of the proposed party meet which had been called to launch the nationwide programme. But what goes beyond one's understanding is the alacrity with which the party called off such an important event. This raises doubts in the minds of many whether this party is really committed to meaningful decentralisation of power at the village level or not. Unfortunately, the Congress(I)'s track record in this respect has been dismal if not hypocritical.

The Congress party leaders' allergy to panchayati raj did not begin just yesterday. It is well known that even when the constitution was being framed, they had expressed their disdain for panchayats. J. D. Sethi (1989) has argued that Congress leaders at the time of our independence were opposed to panchayats. He writes that when these leaders went to meet Gandhiji, to tell him the gist and the main thrust of the proposed constitution, he asked them about the role that had been given to the panchayats.

> These leaders tried to sidetrack the issue. In one of his rare, curt remarks Gandhiji asked them never to come to him for discussion on the constitution again if panchayats were not going to be one of the central pillars of Indian democracy! Embarrassed, these leaders promised Gandhiji they would make panchayats an important part of the constitution. But Gandhiji's assassination proved a very convenient ploy for them to forget it (1989, 27: 15).

Jawaharlal Nehru, however, soon realised that without active local bodies nothing would move below the state level. So, in order to distinguish the new system from the ancient localised system, Nehru coined the term "panchayati raj." The term was meant to convey the sense of panchayati raj as a process and a system of governance, one that transcends the limits of a geographical area. But Nehru's hope that panchayati raj would constitute "the most revolutionary and historical step in the context of new India" was shot down by his own party men.

All analyses show that the critical factor for the success of panchayati raj institutions is political will. Evidence suggests that there were deliberate plans by political leaders, in collusion with the bureaucracy and local vested interests, to emasculate and eventually discard panchayati raj. The ruling Congress party had no qualms when the ministry of community development was reduced to the status of a department and brought under the ministry of food and agriculture. In 1971 the very title "community development" was dropped and replaced by "rural development." "This was not just a cosmetic change," remarked Jain (et al. 1985). "It marked the end of both 'community' and 'panchayats' as agents of change and agencies of development." When the Congress government was thus systematically erasing panchayati raj from the country, there was not even a whimper of protest from the Congress party leaders or from the party's rank and file.

Ironically enough, this situation prevailed only in the Congress ruled states. The states ruled by non-Congress parties had begun to revitalise panchayati raj. Analysing this state of affairs, Govind Narain (1989) made some perceptive remarks which are worth mentioning here. According to him, when the panchayati raj movement was gaining strength and momentum in the early sixties, "A time came when phoney leaders imposed by the political parties found in this programme a danger to their authority and influence and word went round that some elections were lost by the ruling political party in areas in which the programme was strong" (1989: 34). He went on to say that the political will to implement the recommendations of the Balwantrai Mehta committee had been lacking because of the misapprehension that competing centres of influence and power may be created.

One may say that all this is past history and in the post-1985 period, under a new leadership, the Congress(I) has shown a single-minded commitment to the revitalisation of panchayati raj institutions. Public memory is not so short as to forget what the Congress party, under the late Rajiv Gandhi's leadership, did in Tripura in 1988 when talks of enacting a constitutional amendment to include panchayati raj in the statutes were under way.

The first major decision of the Congress(I)-Tripura Upajati Juba Samiti (TUJS) coalition government was to supersede the 704 panchayats in the state and in their place appoint nominated members. This was done by reducing the term of the panchayats from five to four years. Panchayats were replaced by advisory boards comprising nominated Congress(I) members with the promise of holding fresh elections within three months, but nothing came of this. A report from Agartala had stated that, in fact, the Congress(I)-TUJS government had not left intact any grassroots-level democratic organisation. The block development committees had been reconstituted with Congress(I) nominees. The Agartala municipality, the only one of its kind in the state, had also been superseded. The government had been trying to make the autonomous district council its next target but had been restrained by the Supreme Court.

Will any person who is convinced of the importance of grassroots democratic institutions, in his capacity as the president of the ruling party and the prime minister of the country, allow his party to do this in any state? It is also too early to forget that immediately after the imposition of President's Rule in Karnataka on 21 April 1989, the first demand of a certain Congress(I) leader was that the zilla parishads and mandal panchayats in the state be dismantled. Therefore, did not the much trumpeted 64th constitutional amendment of 1989 represent more of political expediency than conviction about and commitment to panchayati raj?

What happened in the Congress-ruled states when the party was returned to power at the centre in 1991 is well known. In Karnataka, elections to panchayati institutions, which were due in the first week of January 1992, were not held (only the elections to the gram panchayats were held on 29 December 1993) despite severe strictures against the government's action by the High Court and Supreme Court. And this story has been repeated in Andhra Pradesh. There the mandala praja parishads, which were established with the aim of taking administration "to the doorstep of the poorest of the poor" through the panchayati raj institutions, were disliked by the Congress(I). The Congress(I) government in Andhra Pradesh dragged its feet on the issue of holding the local bodies elections, which were due in March 1992, even though the High Court and Supreme Court interventions in the matter had become well known. In Kerala the much acclaimed district councils were rendered powerless as soon as the state came under Congress(I) rule with K. Karunakaran as chief minister. While all these things were happening, the central leadership of the party did not as much as lift a finger nor was any hue and cry raised over the systematic destruction of panchayati raj institutions in these states. The party was merely content with the introduction of the 72nd constitution amendment bill in parliament.

The arguments thus far advanced by several political analysts regarding threats from various quarters to the functioning and flourishing of panchayati raj, hold true even after the enactment of the 73rd amendment. There is yet another factor that needs to be taken cognisance of, that is, the provision in the amendment for reservation of one-third seats for women in the elected bodies. This empowerment of women has tremendous potential for radical changes in the rural areas and within the panchayati raj institutions. The vested interests, the bureaucracy and the traditional male-centred political power system in various regions are unlikely to favour this provision. Will the Congress(I) functionaries tolerate this revolutionary change? They know that most women have better common sense and a no-nonsense approach in public life than men. So the very hand that now gives women power through panchayati raj institutions may turn out to be the hand that will sabotage that empowerment.

Way back in 1959, the then deputy chairman of the Planning Commission, the late D.R.Gadgil, had remarked that the prevailing mood was to talk about village democracy but deny real power even to the states. The Congress(I) has only perfected this art of double-speak. But now, will the Congress(I) be able to usher in effective panchayati raj and blaze a new trail?

Response of CPI(M), TDP and Janata

It is ironical that while the Congress party disassociated itself from that which Gandhiji had considered the essence of independent India's strength and vitality, the non-Congress governments adopted as an article of faith. The non-Congress governments regarded panchayati raj as the most vibrant instrument for giving power to the people. When the Janata party came to power at the centre in 1977 it appointed the Asoka Mehta committee to go into the entire question of panchayati raj. As has been noted, the committee's report constituted a landmark in the history of panchayati raj. Although the Janata government did not last long enough to carry out its recommendations, the light kindled did not die out completely. Several non-Congress governments re-organised their moribund panchayati raj system on the basis of this report. This is no mean achievement.

The West Bengal government, led by the CPI(M), was the first to take panchayats seriously, and on 4 June 1978 about twenty-five million rural voters exercised their franchise in order to elect fifty-six thousand panchayat representatives. West Bengal was the only silver lining for quite some time after 1978 on the otherwise dark horizon of centralised power in India. Karnataka followed suit when in 1983 the Janata government passed the bill which radically devolved power to the grassroots level. Karnataka had derived inspiration from West Bengal's experience. (A legislative committee had visited West Bengal in 1983 to study the working of panchayats there.) The Karnataka bill was so revolutionary that when it was sent for the president's approval at the end of 1983, it had to wait more than nineteen months to receive his assent.

Evidently Congress(I) functionaries had realised that only non-Congress governments were taking the initiative for genuine devolution of power and naturally this showed the Congress(I) in a bad light. But the party's pre-occupation with power at the centre at any cost came in the way of its taking any firm steps for giving power to the people. And when, in 1987, 12.5 million rural voters of Karnataka went to the polls to elect their mandal panchayats and zilla parishads, it was another milestone on the road to gram swaraj.

The Telugu Desam government in Andhra Pradesh was the third to accept the recommendations of the Asoka Mehta committee. The party's election manifesto had articulated the importance of panchayati raj. The elections to the mandal praja parishads in 1987 had been a significant step. The Andhra Pradesh act does not go as far as the West Bengal or Karnataka acts. However, its importance lies in that this government boldly went ahead with its promises. Farooq Abdullah, as the chief minister of Jammu and Kashmir, initiated a discussion on decentralisation of power in the state on the lines envisaged in the Asoka Mehta committee report, and brought about the 1989 act. In Kerala, the elections of 1984 were shunned by the Congress(I), and the Left Democratic Front government eventually held them as soon as it came to power.

On 5 August 1986, the then prime minister had written to all the chief ministers requesting them to hold regular elections to panchayati raj bodies. Nothing substantial emerged out of his writing to the Congress(I) ruled states.

Political parties have a vital role to play in developing these political nurseries and it was but natural that the elections in West Bengal, Karnataka and Andhra Pradesh for local bodies be held on party lines. A new culture of elected representatives is slowly but steadily emerging, despite difficulties in getting the cooperation of the bureaucracy. West Bengal has achieved this new culture in a significant way but in Karnataka officialdom is yet to reconcile itself to serving its village masters.

A vibrant local self-government system is the best way to combat natural calamities and crises like floods and drought. Mobilisation of manpower is the key to its success. Relief measures through officials and district administration have inherent limitations. In West Bengal, for instance, the 1978 flood was effectively handled by the newly elected panchayati raj bodies, to the appreciation of all. Again, the panchayat bodies were mainly instrumental in 1978-79 in the speedy reconstruction of the flood-hit areas. Several states would have been spared the agony today if only they had the active gram swaraj visualised by Gandhiji. Gandhiji's concept of gram swaraj would not have been able to become a reality without a constitutional amendment whereby the district administration and the institutional bodies below it were given the necessary powers and regular elections made mandatory. Of course, to achieve this, political resolution was found wanting at the crucial period.

14

The National Front

The National Front's commitment to bring about genuine devolution of power below the state level through the panchayati raj institutions, when it came to power at the centre in 1989, was to be reinforced by the action plan the government had announced. The plan had stated that during the 1990 budget session of parliament, the government would introduce a comprehensive constitution amendment bill on panchayati raj.

Another significant step, taken in a related area, was the preparation for the establishment of an inter-state council. The National Front government straightway started the process of eliciting the views of the state governments on the nature of the duties to be performed by the inter-state council and on its organisation and procedures. But the council itself was to be set up after the ensuing elections in various states.

I would like to argue that, in view of the National Front's and its constituents' basic faith that genuine federalism alone can broaden and deepen the bonds of the unity and integrity of our country, the above schedule was like putting the cart before the horse: the inter-state council ought to have been formed first and then the panchayati raj bill drafted and introduced in parliament, after a thorough discussion in the inter-state council.

Panchayati raj should be a corollary of the federal nature of the Indian polity and not vice versa. The folly committed by the Congress(I) had been to introduce panchayati raj as a cosmetic change (by introducing the 64th constitutional amendment) with scant respect for the structural changes required in the federal functioning of the polity. In other words, the Congress(I) was in a hurry to sell panchayati raj to the voters without fully realising the implications of the constitutional changes it had proposed for the emerging federal spirit of the country. Of course, since decentralisation, both in its profession and practise, has never been the strong point of the Congress(I), one need not be surprised that its bill to amend the constitution, running into eight pages, deflected from genuine devolution of powers. Therefore the move boomeranged. The measures successively adopted by the National Front government to ensure the health of local bodies should not be allowed to meet the same fate.

The accusation of the then opposition party leaders, led by V.P. Singh, that the sudden Congress(I) move to amend the constitution was a gimmick for the ensuing parliamentary elections, was not mere political rhetoric but based on experiences in the states of West Bengal, Karnataka and Andhra Pradesh, and on the meticulously done homework of the opposition parties on decentralisation. The report of the committee appointed by V.P. Singh under the chairmanship of S.R. Bommai on 13 June 1989, to examine the 64th Constitution Amendment Bill in the light of the Janata Dal's approach to democratic decentralisation, is a seminal document setting out certain parameters on the subject. As a member of this committee this author was also involved in the formulation of its report. The conclusions arrived at by the committee (it submitted the report on 10 July 1989) will have an important bearing on the future federal polity of India, in the context of our renewed commitment to revitalise local self-government bodies. The following critical observations of the committee on the 64th Constitution Amendment Bill may be noted:

1. The bill, even within its limited ambit, contained a mass of details which should have been left to legislation by the states in the light of local circumstances obtaining in each state. The bill, therefore, amounts to undue imposition of uniformity on the states for it contains provisions about such matters as how the constituencies should be delimited or how chairpersons of the panchayats should be elected. A constitutional amendment–on a subject primarily concerning the states–should have confined itself to bare essentials.
2. The bill proceeded on the entirely unwarranted assumption that it would be possible for the states to pass down to the panchayats a viable administrative and financial devolution package without the centre doing anything about centre-state relations. Meaningful decentralisation below the state level can

take place only in conjunction with an equally meaningful decentralisation from the centre to the states.

3. At the heart of the decentralisation issue is the pressing need for a new financial regime between the centre, the states and sub-state units of self-government, whether they be rural panchayats or local bodies in urban areas. While governments at each level must raise resources on their own to the extent of the powers available to them, the relatively strong financial position deliberately allotted to the centre by the constitution makes it imperative that there should be a rational scheme of financial devolution from the centre downwards which strengthens democratic self-governance at all levels. The constitution should guarantee that a minimum of 50 percent of the centre's aggregate revenue resources should devolve to the states, and similarly, a minimum of 50 percent of each state's aggregate revenue resources should devolve to panchayats and urban local bodies.

4. There should be a rational arrangement for the sharing of resources available to governments through market borrowing. The best way to do so would be to set up a national credit council composed of representatives of central and state governments, the Reserve Bank of India and the national Planning Commission, with full authority to decide how such sharing should take place.

5. There must be a new planning regime under which planning is viewed as a "national" rather than a "central" activity. The Planning Commission should pay more attention to major policy questions, including hitherto excluded matters like the right balance between defence and development. In regard to state plans, the Planning Commission should confine itself to overall dimensions and their major segments relating to infrastructure, such as power, major irrigation and communications. There must be an end to planning from above. State plans, in particular, should be built from below, the area plans of panchayats and urban local governments forming the base.

6. Cooperatives were recognised from the beginning of the planning era as companion institutions to panchayats, that is, as instruments of economic democracy. The essence of a cooperative organisation is that it must be controlled democratically by its members. The report of the committee on

cooperative law (1987) needs to be made public so that cooperatives can be infused with fresh life after a full national debate.

7. Two important aspects, that is, the pivotal role of the Gram Sabha, comprising all eligible voters in a village, and that of the Nyaya Panchayat for dispensing speedy justice to the people at the village level, find no mention in the bill. The states would be well advised to give due place to these two basic institutions in their legislations.

8. The state legislatures should ensure that elected units of self-government, panchayats or urban local bodies, are squarely in control of the administrative staff dealing with functions devolved on them.

9. If there is a case for reservation for women in the panchayats, and the committee favours reservation of one-third seats for them, there is an equally valid case for similar reservation for women not only in urban local government but also in the state legislatures and in parliament.

10. The move to extend the jurisdiction of the Election Commission to panchayat elections is commendable but steps should be taken to make this constitutional authority more independent. To achieve this, the commission should have the right and duty to report to parliament and the state legislatures on the conduct of elections at different levels. This would generate healthy debate on the problems encountered and the remedies, if any, suggested by the commission, without the central government standing in the way.

11. The move to extend the jurisdiction of another constitutional authority, the Comptroller and Auditor-General of India, is also commendable. In order that he too may be vested with greater independence, his reports should be submitted directly to parliament and the state legislatures. Experience has shown that inconvenient reports are not promptly placed before parliament or the state legislatures, thus offending the principle of open governance and denying to the people the corrective that might be available for a timely and open debate.

The report's salient concerns were succinctly incorporated in the National Front Manifesto which had stated, in unmistakable terms, that the Front wanted the panchayati raj institutions to become instruments through which people could fully participate in the developmental process and that it would promote genuine devolution of powers, functions and resources to local bodies below the state level.

It is pertinent to note that in the National Front Manifesto itself, panchayati raj came within the context and as a consequence of a series of steps enunciated for strengthening the federal nature of the nation, like activating the National Development Council, giving constitutional status to the Planning Commission, reappraisal of Article 356 of the constitution, redefinition of the role of the governors of states and devolution of adequate financial and administrative powers to the states. The first and foremost among these steps was the establishment of an inter-state council under Article 263 of the constitution. The Bommai committee had said in unmistakable terms that the process of strengthening the panchayats and local bodies had to start with the centre withdrawing from those areas which constitutionally belong to the states. The situation warranted a fundamental reappraisal of the entire system of governance. The first step was to restore to the states the dignity and political authority which they had lost under Congress rule. Positive steps must be taken to endow the states with administrative authority and the financial resources necessary to enable them to discharge their constitutional role. In the concurrent sector, the policy must be that no decisions are taken by the centre without full consultation with the states.

The inter-state council is the ideal forum for consultations between the centre and the states as well as between the states. The constitution has laid down critical duties for an inter-state council, including making recommendations on centre-state and inter-state disputes and coordinating policy and action in these areas. The Sarkaria commission also underlined a crucial role for the inter-state council and recommended that it be established under the nomenclature "Inter-Governmental Council." Nirmal Mukarji, supporting the Sarkaria commission's suggestion for an inter-governmental council, argued perceptively that such a council must have an independent, research-based secretariat headed by someone who is more a statesman than a bureaucrat, with the status of a secretary-general, and that he/she should be an important functionary of the home or finance ministry. Mukarji has rightly pointed out that the inter-governmental council is the right forum to consider the recommendations of the Sarkaria commission, the Ninth Finance Commission, and that decentralisation below the state level should be a fit subject for the inter-governmental council, in order to evolve a national consensus on the type of constitutional amendment needed. So the primacy appears to be for creating new normative conditions for the federal structure and not for panchayati raj.

According to the Bommai committee, at the heart of the decentralisation issue is the pressing need for a new financial regime. The relatively strong financial position deliberately allotted to the centre by the constitution, made it imperative that there be a rational scheme of financial devolution from the centre downwards which would strengthen democratic self-governance at all levels. An appropriate constitutional provision was seen as a necessity for a new financial regime. All other aspects should be left to the states to legislate, taking into consideration their historical developments as well as the unique social and cultural situations.

While the National Front government was grappling with the need for revamping the federal structure and also holding discussions with the BJP, the CPI(M), and other friendly parties on the constitution amendment bill, there were hopes that the Uttar Pradesh Janata Dal government would introduce a radical panchayati raj bill which would give teeth to the local bodies. Uttar Pradesh, with 131 million people and sixty-three districts, should become a federation of districts. What the Congress could not do in forty years to empower the democratic institutions at the grassroots level and ensure people's participation in governance, could have been achieved by the Janata Dal with its commitment and political will. Such a measure of lasting value, in consonance with the second generation panchayati raj institutions, which had seen their beginnings in West Bengal and Karnataka, would have been the first of its kind in the Hindi heartland.

(This article was written on 4 December 1989.)

15

Left Democratic Front in Kerala

The Kerala District Council elections of 29 January 1991 could be considered trend-setters in the emerging political scenario in the state and in the country as well. The sweeping victory of the CPI(M)-led Left Democratic Front had made its rank and file optimistic about the next assembly elections (held in early 1992).[1] On the national level, the Janata Dal had noted in its political resolution that the maturing alliance of left and democratic forces had already achieved a "great victory." When, out of fourteen district councils in Kerala, the LDF got a majority in twelve, and lost in one for want of just one seat, it had every reason to be jubilant. The Congress(I)-led United Democratic Front got a majority in the Muslim Malappuram District, but there it was more of a Muslim League victory. The elections dealt a severe blow to the Congress(I) morale.

For all practical purposes the two fronts in Kerala work like a bi-party system. Marginal differences in the voting pattern can make or mar a government. In the 1982 elections, the UDF got just ninety-six thousand votes more than the LDF and the Congress(I)-led ministry ruled the state till 1987. In the last assembly elections, the LDF secured a lead of 150,000 votes and now the LDF has increased its support base–it got 650,000 more votes than the UDF. The reduction in the voting age was partly responsible for this.

In other words, the District Council elections saw the LDF increasing its voting percentage from 44.97 percent (1987) to 47 percent and the UDF's percentage declining from 43.97 (1987) to 40 percent. This was the second time that the LDF was routing the Congress(I) led front in a statewide election; the first time was in 1967 when the Left Front won 111 seats in the 133-member state assembly.

It was said at that time that the Congress(I) was not ready to face a national election. This was true for the party in Kerala also as regards the District Council elections of 1991, and this lack of courage had sent the wrong signals to the people at a crucial time. The people realised that the party and its allies were looking for an excuse to put off the elections. In the natural course, since the LDF had been in power for about four years, the Congress(I) ought to have been in an advantageous position to expose the "misrule" of the ruling group. Moreover, Kerala has a tradition of not voting a party to power for the second time in succession. But unfortunately, the Congress(I) was debilitated because of groupism and uneasy relations with its partners. The party's "high command culture" was not well taken by the Kerala public.

The discomfiture of the Kerala Congress (Mani group) in not getting a berth in the Chandra Shekhar ministry at the centre and its accusations against the Congress(I) leadership in this regard became a butt of ridicule in the popular mind. This sentiment was further fanned by satirists and cartoonists whose influence in opinion-making in the state is second to none.

The Congress(I)'s ambivalence on national issues like the Mandal Commission report and the Ayodhya dispute also cost the party dear. No less important was the party's support to a government headed by Chandra Shekhar which, according to popular perception in Kerala, had no legitimacy, credibility or mandate.

The Nayanar ministry (of the LDF) was not the most efficient one the state had seen till date, but Nayanar had personally carved a niche for himself in the hearts of the Malayalees through his childlike simplicity. The government too had charted a new course with its austerity, sincerity to poll pledges, and a corruption-free administration. All these factors had endeared the government to the people.

Another factor which helped the LDF was the V.P. Singh factor. Keralites believed that V.P. Singh had given up power for the sake of upholding the twin principles of social justice and secularism. They believed that he had paid a heavy price for firmly stopping the foundation stone-laying ceremony of a theocratic state. Thus they felt that by arresting the BJP leader, L.K. Advani, and halting his menacing "Rath Yatra," Singh had been pacifying the growing fear of Muslims and Christians (who together form more than 40 percent of the population in the state) emanating from the terror unleashed by the BJP and its front organisations. The Hindus in Kerala also did not see any virtue in the BJP's new mission and they stood by their Muslim and Christian brethren.

The BJP put up 447 candidates (the total number of seats were 473) but won only two. It polled about 900,000 votes or 6.5 percent of the total votes polled. This is the same percentage the party secured during the assembly elections. On an average, each candidate got two to three thousand votes. If in Trivandrum, Trichur and Calicut districts the BJP got about 100,000 votes each, in Idukki it could gather only twenty-two thousand votes. A section of the affluent among the upper castes remained the only support base for the BJP, thus frustrating its all-India attempts to drive a wedge between the Hindus and the other religious communities with the hindutva slogan.

No party can make an impact on Indian politics without the support of the Backward Classes and the Scheduled Castes. In the Kerala elections the Backward Classes and Scheduled Castes' support to the LDF came in full measure. This swing had begun with the reception the All-Kerala Backward Class Committee had accorded to V.P. Singh just four days before he was defeated in parliament on 9 November 1990, and it had continued unabated throughout his extensive tour of Kerala in December. The message of the Mandal Commission had apparently gone deep into all the *avarna* (untouchable) castes in the state. The turn out in the elections was 73.1 percent, slightly lower by Kerala standards but a very high percentage indeed. The UDF had tried its level best to postpone the elections because of the Gulf war but the LDF did not yield. The people had proved that although they were immensely concerned about their near and dear ones in the Gulf (there was hardly any family in Kerala which was not affected by the Gulf crisis) that fact in itself could not deter them from actively participating in the democratic process.

The high levels of literacy, universal education and political consciousness had created a social milieu for the increased participation of women in decision-making bodies. It is a known fact that Kerala has more women than men. Thus, women voters outnumbered men. In conformity with the National Front's Manifesto, the state had reserved 30 percent seats for women. But in reality many women contested the general seats also.

With the District Council elections, Kerala has joined those states which have implemented the second generation panchayati raj–West Bengal, Karnataka and in some ways Andhra Pradesh. The period following the Asoka Mehta committee report witnessed an attempt to make panchayats political, or units of self-government, as against the earlier concept of panchayats as development agencies.

The Karnataka model had so far been considered the most radical one and now Kerala's model goes beyond the former. In Kerala about 150 subjects have been transferred to the district councils. Those who live in remote areas will not have to go to Trivandrum to get their work done. So if the district councils begin to function smoothly, Kerala will soon be a federation of districts.

(This article was written in February 1991 following the District Council elections in Kerala.)

Note

1. The Kerala Assembly elections were due in May 1992 but because of the overwhelming success of the ruling LDF in the District Council elections in March 1991, the assembly was dissolved. In the elections held in June 1991, the LDF was defeated and the UDF came to power.

Part Five

Critical Issues

16

Women in Panchayati Raj: Beginning of a Silent Revolution

But you cannot draw the masses into politics without drawing the women into politics as well. For, the female half of the human race is doubly oppressed under capitalism...[and] in "household bondage"

–V. I. Lenin

India is perhaps the first country to recognise this social fact underlined by Lenin on the International Working Women's Day in 1921, and to have taken concrete measures to draw women into leadership positions and thereby into politics by giving them one-third reservation in what may now be called the third tier of governance–the panchayati raj. The Constitution (Seventy-third Amendment) Act, 1992, Article 243D(3) reads:

> Not less than one-third (including the number of seats reserved for women belonging to the Scheduled Castes and the Scheduled Tribes) of the total number of seats to be filled by direct election in every Panchayat shall be reserved for women and such seats may be allotted by rotation to different constituencies in a Panchayat.

And Clause (4) of the act has the following provision:

> ...not less than one-third of the total number of offices of Chairpersons in the Panchayats at each level shall be reserved for women:
> Provided also that the number of offices reserved under this clause shall be allotted by rotation to different Panchayats at each level.

The constitutional amendment providing one-third representation to women in elected bodies as well as reserving one-third of the offices of chairpersons for them will have far-reaching consequences in Indian political and social life. This is indeed a welcome, though delayed, gesture for we cannot make democracy meaningful in a traditional society like ours without the full involvement of women. But a constitutional provision is only a necessary step which should be followed by effective measures for women's uplift in the country. To make women's participation in society and politics a reality, enormous work remains to be done, given their present socio-economic condition.

As is well known, if we take the age-specific death rate for children between 0 to 4 years, the male infant mortality rate is 33.6 percent, while the female infant mortality rate touches 36.8 percent, as per the 1987 data. The sex ratio (1991) is one of the lowest with 929 females for every one thousand males. The female literacy rate (1991) is only 39.42 percent when compared to 63.86 percent for males. The work-force participation rate (1991) for males is 51.56 percent and for females, less than half, that is, 22.73 percent. Although all the above mentioned indicators bear a certain degree of relationship, two key socio-economic indicators in particular–the literacy rate and the work-force participation rate–amply testify to the male bias in our society.

The question to be tackled is: Is the removal of these hurdles a must for women's participation in society and the polity? Or will their participation in societal affairs through the panchayati raj institutions remove those handicaps which exist at present? There is no clear-cut answer except to say that we must begin somewhere. And now the seventy-third constitutional amendment gives us a wonderful opportunity to make that beginning. I would argue that sooner than later 50 percent of elected positions in the panchayati raj institutions must be reserved for women, and the state legislatures and parliament should follow this principle.

The Experience of Women in Karnataka

Before the historic Karnataka Zilla Parishads, Taluk Panchayat Samitis, Mandal Panchayats and Nyaya Panchayats Act, 1983 (with 25 percent reservation for women) was implemented in 1987, women's entry into panchayats was only possible through the nomination of one or two women to these bodies.

For instance, in Maharashtra, out of the 320 women representatives of panchayat samitis and zilla parishads in 1978, 314 were nominated! And Maharashtra is considered one of the few states which has satisfactorily implemented the panchayati raj system in the wake of the Balwantrai Mehta committee report of 1957.

A study of the women elected representatives to Karnataka panchayati raj institutions between 1987 and 1990, conducted by the Institute of Social Sciences, gives an insight into women's present position in the panchayats as elected members and the possibilities this holds for the future. The study also gives an insight into the nature of their participation, their present sociological and cultural compulsions and their leadership role in society. Since it has an all-India bearing, it is important to go into these findings in some detail.

The study revealed that women from the dominant castes–the Lingayats and Vokkaligas–formed 60 percent of the elected women members in the zilla parishads in Karnataka. It may be mentioned here that these two castes constituted 50.61 percent of all the members in the zilla parishads. In Karnataka, women had contested only for the seats reserved for them and not for the general ones. The 1983 act provided for at least one Scheduled Caste woman to be represented in each Zilla Parishad.

There was a predominance of younger members among the women compared to that among men. More than three-fourths of the women Zilla Parishad members were below forty-five years and more than half the members were in the age group of twenty-five to thirty-five. Incidentally, Karnataka was the first state to lower the voting age to eighteen. It is said that political parties had considerable difficulty in finding women candidates but found it easier to persuade younger women to enter public life than the older generation because of the latter's conservative and traditional outlook. This also means that the candidates were relatively inexperienced in politics and public life. Almost 80 percent of the women members in the Zilla Parishad had no experience of active politics, except for exercising their franchise in a few elections. The remaining 20 percent had served either in the erstwhile panchayats or in taluk development boards. And this 20 percent included two former M.L.As also.

The women who contested the 1987 elections were very often the relatives of political leaders. Usually a male member of the family had been instrumental in persuading the women to contest. During the election campaign, these women were always projected as someone's wife, mother, sister or widow, as the case may be. They attributed their victory in the elections to the political party or its leader or the status of the male member of the family. None mentioned their own potential or promises. By and large, these women candidates were unknown in their constituencies. The women Zilla Parishad members were not sensitive to party identities and loyalties, unlike their male counterparts. "We are not interested in party politics!" they would insist.

The participation of women in the Zilla Parishad meetings was also an eye-opener. If any woman wished to raise any issue, she chose to speak about it to the adhyaksha or the upadhyaksha, after the meeting when the male members would be leaving the hall. Quite often a male member would also be there to support her. Women members from the southern and coastal districts of Karnataka were more vocal than those from the northern districts because of the former's exposure to the urban situation and also due to cultural factors. The social distance in the presence of men, and the relative inexperience and uncertainty as to what they say would be acceptable or not, often came in the way of the women's participation in the meetings. Most women members did not visit the Zilla Parishad offices except when attending meetings. Occasionally the men escorted the women members and also accompanied them to the meeting hall, prompting them to speak. A case, oft cited, is that of the husband of an elected woman wanting to speak on behalf of his wife in the Zilla Parishad meetings.

In education, women elected members lagged behind men. While 20 percent of the men in the zilla parishads had professional and post graduate education, women with comparable qualifications totalled only 5 percent. A majority of women members gave their occupation as agriculture, housework and social work. Most women preferred to indicate their profession as housewives. With their entry in panchayats, women had acquired the additional responsibility of public life along with household work. Some women found the conflicting roles a strain on their time and resources. This caused a feeling of guilt that they had not been able to fulfill their obligations to their families. In many cases women continued to have all their time for household chores as usual, because the men in their families were involved in discharging the political responsibilities on their behalf. It has been observed that after they get elected, women are no longer considered in terms of caste. The fact that they are women takes precedence over all other aspects of social identity. These findings were based on the field studies done at a time when the zilla parishads had just come into being.

After about two years, when the same zilla parishads were studied, changes were evident. More women were expressing themselves; they had an opinion on various matters that came up for discussion. A qualitatively improved participation in terms of the contents of their comments was also evident. Many women members were taking interest in acquiring a better knowledge of the working of zilla parishads. It was also noticed that the women representatives and office bearers were not corrupt and they had a no-nonsense approach in dealing with education, health, hygiene and such matters which come under the purview of panchayats.

What the Karnataka study shows is that women have social handicaps and constraints of various kinds in functioning effectively but with experience their effectiveness improves. Moreover, as more and more regular elections take place, the independence of women will increase; they will not be depending on their male family members for support or identity. Over the decades, the electoral process and thereby the grassroots-level democratic process has been throttled and women's innate abilities have not been allowed to blossom. From this point of view what has been initiated through the seventy-third constitutional amendment is the beginning of a silent revolution.

Female Literacy and Panchayats

One of the most important preconditions for this silent revolution to be successful is women's education. The states which have given importance to women's education have shown phenomenal increases in all indicators of social progress, like a lower birth rate, higher health standards as well as a higher expectation of life at birth. Thus, women's participation in public life and their leadership has a direct link with the above factors.

The Institute of Social Sciences had conducted another study in 1991, this time of the social background of District Council members in Kerala. The results of this study pertaining to women members are a pointer to these issues under discussion.

The Kerala district councils have 474 seats. When the study was conducted the effective strength of the district councils was 472, and 78 percent of those questioned all over the state had responded. Out of these, 126 were women–that is, 34 percent of the total interviewed. The percentage of women elected in the council elections was far above the mandatory 30 percent reservations made for them in the state in 1991. It meant that a large number of women had fought against men in non-reserved constituencies, and had won.

All the members interviewed were literate. Out of the total members interviewed, 51 percent were graduates, 13 percent were post-graduates and only 7 percent had studied up to primary school. All members claimed that they read newspapers. Eighty-three percent read more than two newspapers, 11 percent read two newspapers and 3 percent read one newspaper a day.

Secular ideas have also made deep inroads. A thirty-seven year old woman respondent from Malabar said that she had received education up to the tenth class. She reads more than two newspapers a day, and is a member of the board of the District Cooperative Bank and the cooperative society. She refused to indicate the caste to which she was born!

Taking the situation in the country as a whole, women's educational levels are abysmally low, to say the least. After forty-six years of independence, the literacy rate of women in some states is almost at the same point as it was when we began our journey in 1947. In 1951 the female literacy rate was a mere 8.86 percent. Over the years, however, there had been a steady improvement, as it had moved up to 39 percent in 1991. But noticeably, while the literacy rate had gone up, the total number of illiterates had also increased.

If we take the case of two southern states–Karnataka and Tamil Nadu–the female literacy rate in rural areas for the age group of fifteen and above is only 18.6 percent in Karnataka and 23.6 percent in Tamil Nadu. The comparative figures in the urban areas are 51.7 percent and 57.4 percent, in Karnataka and Tamil Nadu respectively. Tamil Nadu has a better literacy rate in comparison to Karnataka. And the percentage of girls attending schools in Karnataka between the age group of ten to fourteen is only 37.8, while in Tamil Nadu it is slightly better, being 44.6 percent. This means that about 62 percent of the girls in Karnataka and 55 percent of the girls in Tamil Nadu in this age-group are *not* attending schools today.

Is it lack of resources which keep many states in this position? Is it lack of personnel? Or is it the lack of political will? Or, to put it differently, is it the vested interests which keep them ignorant and illiterate? In a democracy, votes determine power. Therefore, vote banks which will assure someone's continuance in power are very important. More ignorance and less questioning creates that ideal situation for the vote "bankers." Illiteracy, lack of education are the preconditions for it.

The great Muslim reformer of Algeria, A.Ibn-Badis' (1889-1940) statement on women's education, "Educate a boy and you educate a person. Educate a girl and you educate a nation," can be ignored only at our peril.

Opponents of Reservation for Women

Those who oppose reservation of seats for women in panchayats brandish four main reasons in support of their stand. First, women who become members of panchayats and local bodies will disturb the harmony of homes and of family life. Even those men who tolerate women working in offices for fixed hours do not take kindly to them when their roles change to one of community leadership. This is because then the women have to attend to people's problems as leaders. This means irregular hours of work and a twenty-four hour demand on their time. Therefore, who will look after the children and household chores, the menfolk ask?

Second, women will become targets of attacks by anti-social elements when they move out of their homes or go outside their villages for work, meetings, and so on. A case was cited of one state where a few local women leaders, obliged to spend nights away from home during their travel, were attacked by goons and even raped. Will any male family member allow his wife, daughter or sister to take part in a public role which has such potential dangers, they ask?

Third, they mention that whenever women hold elected offices, the male officers are the ones who "dictate" what is or is not to be done. They take control of the entire situation and women elected representatives become the hapless victims of officialdom.

Finally, these opponents contend, even if women are elected in large numbers, the power equation will never change. "Instead of Ram Singh, Ram Singh's wife will be there," these villagers quip.

Evidently, these and many other problems are the product of a particular mind-set and culture of male dominance. A social transformation aimed at the woman's changing role could be achieved by panchayati raj institutions. But, of course, the task is beset with enormous difficulties for women in its initial phases.

II

The Case of Orissa

The Orissa panchayati raj elections of May-June 1992 had attracted media attention due to reports that they were violent, even bloody, having claimed seventeen lives. The fact that the elections to the municipalities, grama panchayats and panchayat samitis were ushering in a silent social revolution in one of our backward states has been conveniently sidelined. The most significant aspect of the Orissa local bodies elections was the encouragement they gave to women. While other states, in the light of the 72nd constitution amendment bill introduced in parliament in 1991, were only deliberating on the provision of one-third representation to women, Orissa had gone ahead and implemented the provision. Moreover, even among the Scheduled Tribes and Scheduled Castes, for whom reservation has been made proportionate to their population in the Grama Panchayat or the Panchayat Samiti, one-third of the seats are set apart for women. The state has 1,444 municipal and 76,789 panchayat wards. With this progressive aspect of the legislation already implemented in a state where female literacy is only 29.1 percent, to have more than 480 women representatives in the municipalities and twenty-five thousand women representatives in the panchayats is not a small achievement.

Orissa did not stop here. The Orissa Grama Panchayat Act, 1964, was amended in 1992 year to include the provision that in every Grama Panchayat if a sarpanch, elected or nominated, was not a woman, the office of the naib-sarpanch in that Grama Panchayat should be given to a woman. Similar amendment was brought in for the posts of chairpersons of the panchayat samitis. This is a radical step. No other state has such an enabling provision for women to hold office.

Eyebrows were raised when the chief minister, Biju Patnaik, had insisted that one-third seats should be reserved for women. Skeptics (male chauvinists included) told him politely that there would not be enough women candidates to contest all the seats reserved for them and therefore all this was a waste of time. But Biju Patnaik knew the reality on the ground and went ahead with his plans. The skeptics were proved wrong. Out of 1,430 municipal wards to which elections were held, 478 wards had women candidates only and each of these wards had five to ten candidates in the fray. The situation during panchayat elections was no different. In the hotly contested municipal chairpersons posts, women captured four seats which included Bhubaneswar. Biju Patnaik had told women, "As long as I am alive I stand by you and give what is legitimately yours. Grab it and make good use of it." He now regrets that he could not give 50 percent reservation for women in all the elected bodies. In his own characteristic way, he stunned the assembly recently by declaring that he would like to see that 50 percent seats are reserved for women in the legislatures as well!

Biju Patnaik's conviction and enthusiasm to give women their due share in society has at times recoiled on him politically. In the Bhubaneswar Panchayat Samiti elections, the female candidate of the Janata Dal was defeated by the Congress(I)'s Dusharan Swain in spite of the ruling Janata Dal party enjoying a majority. Bhubaneswar is Biju Patnaik's constituency and in the earlier municipal elections, much against the prevailing political mood, he could put up a young, dynamic woman candidate for the municipal chairperson's directly elected post and see to it that she won the contest. That was not to be this time.

The chief minister has a committed panchayati raj minister in a veterinary doctor-turned-politician, Damodar Raut. The chief minister, the panchayati raj minister and the minister for urban affairs, along with their women representatives and women supporters, face heavy odds ahead. The main problem will come from the M.L.As themselves who will be unhappy to share some of their powers and spheres of influence with the leadership at the lower levels. Even the ruling party M.L.As have reservations about giving so much power to panchayats. And if a sizeable number of functionaries in these panchayats are women, then their resentment can be well imagined.

It is to be expected that the M.L.As will employ every conceivable method to sabotage local self-government and prevent it from taking-off. In fact, they had begun this even before the elections. These elections were to be held, for instance, on 15 February 1992, but there was opposition from the M.L.As, who, on one pretext or the other, tried to prevent the elections on this date. The next date for the elections was fixed for the following April. Again objections and arguments were put forward to postpone them. So the third date was fixed for 15 May. When the election process was about to be set in motion, the same lobby again wanted the elections to be postponed, this time to November.

Biju Patnaik had to intervene and say enough is enough. Finally, the elections commenced on 20 May and ended on 7 June. The elections for the posts of Panchayat Samiti chairpersons began on 29 June and were completed in two days. So what lies in store for the panchayats in Orissa, from the vested interests, the bureaucracy, and the M.L.As, who are not convinced of the need for conferring power on these institutions of self-government, may not be different from the experience of some other states. The only answer to the detractors of local self-government is a strong political will and the building of healthy conventions to safeguard the institutions.

No elections, anywhere at the grassroots level, can be free from complaints regarding the use of money or force. But in a backward economy the degree of violence is likely to be directly in proportion to the power the local bodies wield and the frequency with which the elections are conducted. Since the municipal elections were being held in the state after a gap of thirteen years and panchayat elections after nine years, the pent-up feelings and emotions connected with the election process found their expression in violence. Interestingly, an analysis of the incidents of violence shows that most of them occurred during the victory processions. But the fact that repolling was needed only in 368 booths out of about seventy-seven thousand, under normal policing, speaks for itself. Since the elections were on a party basis, the violence was less. After all, the prestige of every party was at stake.

Orissa has taken concrete steps to vest more powers in the local bodies. Along with the already existing subjects, the new amendment has transferred eight important departments like minor forest produce, small-scale industries, including food processing, rural housing, poverty alleviation programmes, women and child welfare, social welfare and the public distribution system. A finance commission has been appointed to strengthen the financial base of these village governments.

When we say that these elections signified a silent revolution, it is not just rhetoric. The participation of the people in the elections was overwhelming. While in the municipal elections more than 50 percent of the voters participated, the panchayat elections saw 75 to 85 percent voting. When we consider that in the assembly elections the average voting is less than 50 percent, we can see that when democracy comes nearer to the people, their participation and enthusiasm increases, making democracy genuine and meaningful.

17

Political Parties in Panchayat Elections

Whether and to what extent political parties should participate in panchayati raj elections is a question that had been at the centre-stage of discussions on panchayati raj in the country even before independence. In fact, the Santhanam committee (1964) set up to study the elections to panchayats, had stated that this had been one of the most controversial issues it found itself dealing with (Government of India 1965: 51). The question has added significance because of the two prominent and at the same time sharply divided schools of thought on the subject of participation of political parties in local bodies elections. One major line of thought advocated apolitical panchayat bodies while the other was against the "woolly idea of having local bodies' elections on an apolitical basis" (Subrahmanyam 1989).

The panchayati raj acts in different states do not say anything about the official participation of political parties in the panchayat elections. For that matter constitutions need not say anything about political parties unless proportional representation is provided for, as, for instance, in the constitution of West Germany. In the constitution of India, parties are mentioned only in terms of the anti-defection clause. However, in the context of opposing schools of thought on the participation of political parties in the "governments" below the state level, and the not too favourable attitude of a major party like the Congress(I) on the subject, this paper attempts to discuss the "route" of this debate and argue that without the official participation of political parties, the panchayats will be democracy in form only, without substance.

The Sarvodaya idea inspired by Gandhiji was that panchayati raj institutions should be "non-political," meaning that political parties should be kept out of panchayat bodies. Consensus was considered the best way of arriving at decisions. Jayaprakash Narayan believed that parties had corrupted the whole of the panchayati raj programme and had used decentralisation for selfish party interests. *Sarvodayees* (supporters of the Sarvodaya movement) wanted to rebuild Indian democracy on the basis of *gram samaj* (village society) at the bottom and upper tiers, that is, at the samiti, district, state and all-India level. Representation at each level would have to be through indirect elections. They believed that in this way, the principle of consensus, if not unanimity, would prevail at all levels of the administration and electioneering and party politics would be eliminated. Of course, this argument had a fine moral appeal. As the vast majority of our people are illiterate and ignorant, the burden of the protagonists of this school was "to save them from becoming pawns in the contest for power by political parties and ambitious pressure groups" (Narayan 1961; Mishra et al. 1967).

Jayaprakash Narayan was critical of political parties because he believed that they impeded self-government and the liberation of local initiative. For Narayan, local self-government cannot be created within a system with competing political parties (Narayan 1961). His ultimate idea was "partyless democracy." In 1961 the All-India Panchayat Parishad, of which JP–as Jayaprakash Narayan was popularly called–was chairman, went to the extent of advising the states to work for uncontested elections, and to give rewards to villages electing their panchayat without contest. About 30 percent of all the panchayat elections at that time were uncontested. The protagonists of the Westminster model of parliamentary democracy considered the non-political, non-party system propagated by the Sarvodaya schools as "visionary." They even suspected that it would lead to totalitarianism.

The liberal democracy school opposed this concept and wanted political participation. S.K. Dey, for instance, characterised democracy without contest as a democracy of dead people. "A self-sufficient village republic consisting of god-fearing people, thinking, believing and acting all alike, is a village dead before it is born. Life cannot spring from such an inanition. Democracy demands ideology and ideals in a perpetual but healthy clash. Only dead people do not compete" (1960: 173). In a conference convened in Jaipur in 1964 to discuss the question of panchayati raj and democracy, there was a clash between those holding these two contesting viewpoints.

S. C. Jain of the Rural Institute Vidya Bhawan supported the Sarvodaya view while C. P. Bhambri and others argued that the involvement of political parties in the panchayati raj system was both necessary and desirable as the parties would act as tools of modernisation in the villages. "The panchayati raj institutions provide a base for progressive parties to operate and fight against the forces of backwardness and tradition. The village people are to be politicised...Political parties have to act as a great instrument for the politicisation of the rural masses" (quoted in Kihlberg 1970).

The Santhanam committee's review of the subject showed that before the advent of independence and in the period soon after, there had been proposals to political parties not to contest municipal elections. Occasionally, all parties have stayed away from such elections but no resolution to abstain had been observed for any length of time. During the Nehruvian period (till 1964), most political parties abstained from direct participation in elections to panchayats. One of the reasons for this was that in small wards with 100 to 500 voters, locally prominent men were likely to succeed. They did not adopt party labels but the political parties used to enroll the elected members into their fold. However, in Tamil Nadu (then Madras), in the panchayat elections in 1964, direct contests were fought between the Congress party and the Communists, with 36.3 percent panchayat members in the state getting elected unopposed, while in Andhra Pradesh 45 percent were elected unopposed.

The use of party symbols in panchayat elections was not permitted in the states (except in Kerala) but even here such symbols were not used at the time of the Santhanam committee review. The committee was of the opinion that while the influence of political parties cannot be legally banned, it was wrong and unnecessary to encourage their entry into the village by providing them party symbols. The committee's recommendations merit our attention because they reflect the thinking at the time. The recommendations were:

1. There should be no legal provision prohibiting political parties from influencing panchayati raj elections.
2. No political party symbol should be issued in any election to panchayati raj institutions.

3. No representations from political parties should be entertained in relation to panchayati raj institutions.
4. Official recognition should not be accorded to political party groupings among members of panchayati raj bodies.

Only the first recommendation was at slight variance with the Sarvodaya stand while all others were in conformity with the Jayaprakash Narayan school. But on the question of unanimity in elections, the committee took a strong stand against the Sarvodaya line, saying "no cash prizes or material inducements or incentives should be offered for unanimity in panchayati raj elections." The committee believed that contests were both healthy and educative and it recorded having come across villages where the anxiety for unanimity and consensus meant the continuing domination of the traditional authorities and the suppression of the new spirit of youth. An experience the committee had in Gujarat was illuminating.

> In Gujarat, we visited a village where the panchayat had been unanimously elected for many terms without any change of personnel. When we put the question whether there were no other persons fit to serve in the panchayat and why the same persons were elected continuously for long periods, the only reply was that no one wanted a change (Government of India 1965: 55).

The conclusions of the Santhanam committee were important for that time. "Contests are both healthy and educative. Avoidance of contests on a large scale may mean the suppression of youth and it may stunt the growth of panchayati raj itself" (1965: 55).

We find a remarkable change after about four years of the Santhanam committee report. At an important conference on panchayati raj in 1969 at Hyderabad, the majority opinion was for political competitiveness on an ideological basis for both rural and urban India. But the dissenting voice at the meet still believed that the intimate, community-type of existence of the Indian village could be better served if it was insulated from political party rivalries.

Soon this theoretical and ideological debate more or less died out. The appointment of the Asoka Mehta committee on 12

December 1977 constituted a watershed in the history of panchayati raj institutions. In its report submitted to Prime Minister Morarji Desai on 21 January 1978 the committee unequivocally stated that political parties should be allowed to participate effectively at all levels:

> [It]...would make for a clearer orientation towards programmes and would facilitate healthier linkages with higher level political processes. It is also necessary to provide a constructive outlet to opposition parties; parties out of power at the state level may be able to chalk out achievements at the district level. Direct elections, coupled with programme-based contests would offer greater scope to the weaker sections for availing of the opportunities offered by the political system (Government of India 1978: 52).

The first state to put into practise the Asoka Mehta committees' suggestions was West Bengal. Nineteen years after the inauguration of panchayati raj in the country, for the first time, political parties were officially recognised in the local elections. But the two Congress parties at that time pleaded for non-partisan panchayat polls. The Janata party was divided on the issue–P. C. Sen strongly opposed party-based contests while Sushil Dhara and Biman Mitra held a different view. The CPI(M) believed that the direct involvement of political parties in the working of panchayati raj institutions would make the panchayat leadership more disciplined and responsible in managing these institutions and would put an end to the age-old tradition of rural coteries reaping the benefits for narrow, sectarian and caste interests. The Left parties countered P. C. Sen's "partyless democracy" thesis with the argument that "partyless candidates could not bring about social change and uphold and strengthen democracy because collective, organised efforts are needed for this; only political parties could bring them about...." (Shiviah et al. 1980: 53).

The Karnataka elections to panchayats in 1987 were held on party lines. For the first time, individuals who had dominated the villages on the basis of their caste, family, money-power and bullying tactics, were challenged by candidates put up by the national or regional parties. Villages which had been subjected to several decades of domination by one particular family or caste, had to face stiff challenges. Of course, the rural scene witnessed serious rifts and restlessness, even among families, whose members were often found to be aligned on different party lines.

The London County Council, for instance, has had from its inception in 1889, clearly defined party divisions between its members. Elections are frequently held on party lines. In the local governments in England, party organisation brings greater coherence and definition into the policies of the governing body. Eric Jackson, in his study of local government in England, came to the following conclusion:

> Political organisation in local government affairs does have the undoubted advantage, as it does in Parliament, of bringing greater coherence and definition into the policy of the governing body. Where the parties are well organised and disciplined, it is possible to get a decision more quickly than when there is no such organisation....The leader of a political group in power or a representative who can speak with authority on behalf of that group, can be much more sure of his touch when conducting such discussions, and those with whom he is discussing can feel that what he says is more likely to be adopted by the council than when discussions are conducted by a representative who has no such backing (1959: 140).

Of course, one can argue that party discipline will necessarily limit the freedom of its members, that real power would tend to drift into the hands of the leading politicians and that party organisation, instead of elected panchayats, may become the real governing body. There are complaints that the CPI(M) in West Bengal, the Janata in Karnataka and the Telugu Desam party in Andhra Pradesh betray these tendencies. But this is not a serious problem because if parties and politicians have to endure, they must be sensitive to public criticism. They have to observe the rules of the game.

In India's particular social and political situation, there may be a tendency among the ruling parties to adopt an ostrich-like policy on parties officially contesting local elections. These elections, at any point of their tenure, are seen as a verdict on the performance and popularity of political parties. More often than not political parties would like to shy away rather than face the test. The panchayat elections held in Uttar Pradesh on 5 June 1988, without the official participation of political parties, are a case in point. In such a context, independent candidates of all hues and shades, claiming the support of one or the other party, and in a free-for-all situation, without any internal control or accountability, are found to be in the fray. It is a well-known fact that the men who attacked the street theatre group led by Safdar Hashmi in Uttar Pradesh owed their allegiance to an independent candidate in the local elections. But it is an open secret that these independents are not so independent. If a party finds that it has no base, it may support an "independent." It is clear to all that the candidate in Hashmi's murder incident was only "independent" on paper, for it was widely reported that the Congress(I), unable to operate in small towns like Ghaziabad, had put up these so-called independents to spread terror.

Only official party participation will prevent lumpens taking over politics. Therefore, the panchayati raj institutions (and their elections) should be seen as nurseries for political leadership. Young blood will be attracted to them if elections are based on political ideology and inspired by the state as well as the national political leadership.

At present, of course, there is dearth of able political leadership at the lower levels. No wonder, therefore, that when national parties had to select candidates for mandal elections in Karnataka, they found it difficult to identify enough party activists. The organic link from Gram Sabha to Lok Sabha can be achieved effectively only if political parties work with the people. The absence of this link has brought about a pathological decay in our democratic system. Wherever official parties have been involved in the panchayats, the enthusiasm of the local people has been high and the percentage of polling unprecedented. For instance, as is well known, in the 1978 West Bengal panchayat elections one of the most important reasons for the widespread popular participation was that political parties were officially involved in the elections. No doubt this decision (to have political party participation) helped considerably in making the rural folk politically conscious, giving elected panchayat bodies a political standing of their own (Mukhopadhay 1991).

Panchayati raj elections, held on a party basis, will certainly heighten the politicisation of the people. Almost all political parties, except the Congress(I), have welcomed the politicisation of the people in panchayati raj elections. It seems that the

Congress(I) is not favourably disposed towards the politicisation of the masses because it fears that this will open the floodgates of demands, and the assertion of rights. This ambiguity of the Congress(I) is not helpful for genuine devolution of power at the grassroots level.

Glossary

Adhyaksha	:	Chairperson
Anchal Panchayat	:	Group of village panchayats in West Bengal
avarna	:	Ritually impure (Untouchable)
Barga	:	Share-cropping
Bargadaar	:	Sharecropper
Dhobi	:	Washerman
Divas	:	Day / Occasion
Gram(a)	:	Village
Grameena	:	Belonging to a village
Gram(a) Sabha	:	Village assembly
Gram(a) Samaj	:	Village society
Gram(a) Swaraj	:	Village republic
Halqa Panchayat	:	Group of village panchayats in Jammu and Kashmir
Harijan	:	Literally, children of god (an appellation used by Gandhiji for the lowest castes)
hindutva	:	Ideology based on resurgent Hindu nationalism
Hoblies	:	Approximately 30 villages, under a revenue inspector below the tahsildar in old Karnataka
Jamaath	:	Organisation
Karmadhyaksha	:	Chairman of Panchayat Standing Committee
Kum Kum	:	Vermilion powder applied on forehead
Lathi	:	A heavy stick
Mahanadu	:	Great assembly (Telugu)
Mandal Panchayat	:	Group of village panchayats in Karnataka covering 10-12,000 persons
Mandal Praja Parishad	:	Tier between Zilla Parishad and Gram Panchayat in Andhra Pradesh
Mathrujati	:	Women who symbolise the essence of motherhood
mu	:	Chinese measure equal to

		one-sixth of an acre
Naib Sarpanch	:	Deputy head of Village Panchayat
Nyaya Panchayat	:	Judicial Panchayat
Panchayat	:	An assembly of five
Panchayat Adalat	:	Panchayat Court
Panchayat Samiti	:	Block Panchayat
Pradhan	:	Elected head of Village Panchayat
Praja	:	People
Puja :	:	Worship
Rashtrapati Bhavan	:	Official residence of the President of India
Sabhadhipati	:	Chairman of District Panchayat in West Bengal
Sadar-e-Riyasat	:	Head of the state of Jammu and Kashmir
Sahakari Sabhadhipati	:	Vice-chairman of Zilla
Sarpanch(a)	:	Elected head of village panchayat
Sarvodaya	:	Literally, emancipation of all. The name of a movement
Shastra Sahitya Parishad	:	Organisation for People's Science Movement in Kerala
Sthayee Samitis	:	Standing committees
swaraj	:	Self-rule
Taluk Panchayat Samiti	:	Tier between District and Mandal Panchayat in Karnataka
Upadhayaksha	:	Vice-chairman
Upajati	:	Scheduled Tribe as in Tripura
Zilla Parishad	:	District Panchayat
Zilla Praja Parishad	:	District Panchayat in Andhra Pradesh
Zilla Abhivrudhi Sameeksha Mandali	:	District Development Review Comittee in Andhra Pradesh

References

Adisheshiah, Malcolm S. 1986. "The need for constitutional safeguards," in George Mathew (ed.), *Panchayati raj in Karnataka today. Its national dimensions.* New Delhi: Concept Publishing Company.

All-India Congress Committee (AICC). 1954. *Report of the Congress village panchayat committee.* New Delhi: AICC.

Asoka Mehta Committee. 1978. *Report of the committee on panchayati raj institutions.* New Delhi.

AVARD (Association of Voluntary Agencies for Rural Development). 1962. *Report of a study team on panchayati raj in Rajasthan.* New Delhi.

Bandyopadhya, Debbrata. 1981. *Land reforms in West Bengal.* Calcutta: Government of West Bengal.

CAARD (Committee to Review the Existing Administrative Arrangements for Rural Development and Poverty Alleviation Programmes). 1985. *Report.* New Delhi: Department of Rural Development, Ministry of Agriculture.

Chandrashekar, B. K. 1984. "Panchayati raj law in Karnataka: Janata initiative on decentralisation," *Economic and Political Weekly* 19 (16).

Datta, A. 1985. "Decentralisation and local government reform in India," *Indian Journal of Public Administration* 31(3).

Dey, S.K. 1961. *Panchayati raj.* 2nd edition, Bombay: Asia Publishing House.

———. 1960. *Community development. A movement is born.* Allahabad: Kitab Mahal.

Dhar, P.N. 1964. "Historical realities," *Seminar* 58 (June).

Gandhi, M.K. 1942. " My idea of village swaraj," *Harijan,* 26 July.

Ghosh, Buddhadeb. 1993. "Relationship between the Zilla Parishad and district bureaucracy. The case of West Bengal." Unpublished manuscript.

Government of India. 1965. *Report of the committee on panchayati raj elections.* New Delhi: Ministry of Community Development.

———. 1960. *From Lok Sabha to Gram Sabha.* New Delhi: Ministry of Community Development and Cooperation.

———. 1958. *A study of panchayats.* New Delhi.

Hirway, Indira. 1990. "At cross roads," in P. Satyanarayana (ed.) *Towards new panchayati raj. Critical perspectives on the reorganisation of rural local government.* New Delhi: Uppal Publishing House.

Imperial Gazetteer of India 4 (1909).

Jackson, W. Eric. 1959. *Local government in England and Wales.* New edition, Middlesex: Penguin Books.

Jain, L.C. et al. 1985. *Grass without roots.* New Delhi: Sage Publications.

Jathar, R.V 1964. *Evolution of panchayati raj in India.* Dharwar: Institute of Economic Research.

Kihlberg, M. 1970. *The panchayati raj of India. Debate in a developing country.* New Delhi: Young Asia.

Maheshwari, B. 1963. *Studies in panchayati raj.* Delhi: Metropolitan Book Company.

Mathew, George (ed.). 1990. *Panchayati raj in Jammu and Kashmir.* New Delhi: Concept Publishing Company.

——. 1987. "Panchayat poll in Karnataka," *The Hindustan Times,* 9 February.

——(ed.). 1986. *Panchayati raj in Karnataka today. Its national dimensions.* New Delhi: Concept Publishing Company.

Mishra, K.P. and R. Avasthi (eds.). 1967. *Politics of Persuasion.* Bombay: P. C. Manaktala & Sons.

Mukhopadhyay, A.K. 1991. *The panchayat administration in West Bengal.* Calcutta: The World Press.

Narain, Govind. 1989. "Panchayati raj–some recollections," *Yojana* 33 (1 & 2).

Narayan, Jayaprakash. 1961. *Swaraj for the people.* Varanasi: Akhil Bharat Sarva Seva Sangh.

Nazir Sab, Abdul. 1986. "Towards a four pillar state," in George Mathew (ed.). *Panchayati raj in Karnataka today. Its national dimensions.* New Delhi: Concept Publishing Company.

Quarterly of the Local Self-Government Institute (A) 128 (1949).

Sarkaria Commission. 1988. *Summary recommendations of the commission on centre-state relations.* New Delhi: Ministry of Home Affairs.

Sen, Amartya. 1986. *Poverty and famines. An essay on entitlement and deprivation.* New Delhi: Oxford University Press.

Sethi, J. D. 1989. "Panchayats: Democracy or Dictatorship?" *Mainstream* 27 (15 July).

Shiviah, M. et al. 1980. *Panchayati raj elections in West Bengal, 1978.* Hyderabad: National Institute of Rural Development (NIRD).

Shukla, L.P. 1964. *A History of village panchayats in India.* Dharwar: Institute of Economic Research.

Singh, Charan. 1981. *Economic nightmare of India: Its cause and cure.* New Delhi: National Publishing House.

Subrahmanyam, K. 1989. "Panchayat reform: A few pitfalls can be avoided," *The Hindustan Times,* 18 May.

Webster, Neil. 1990. "Panchayati raj and the decentralisation of development planning in West Bengal: A case study," CDR Project paper 90.7, Copenhagen: Centre for Development Research (CDR).

Westergaard, Kirsten. 1986. *Peoples participation, local government and rural development: The case of West Bengal.* Copenhagen: Centre for Development Research.

Venkatarangaiya, M., and M. Pattabhiram (eds.). 1969. *Local government in India: Select readings.* Bombay: Allied Publishers.

Index